Contents

BUILT IN THE
U.★S.★A.★

120 224

BUILT IN THE
U★S★A★

AMERICAN BUILDINGS FROM AIRPORTS TO ZOOS

120224

Building Watchers Series

EDITED BY DIANE MADDEX
NATIONAL TRUST FOR HISTORIC PRESERVATION

THE PRESERVATION PRESS

The Preservation Press
National Trust for Historic Preservation
1785 Massachusetts Avenue, N.W.
Washington, D.C. 20036

The National Trust for Historic Preservation is the only private, non-profit national organization chartered by Congress to encourage public participation in the preservation of sites, buildings and objects significant in American history and culture. Support is provided by membership dues, endowment funds, contributions and grants from federal agencies, including the U.S. Department of the Interior, under provisions of the National Historic Preservation Act of 1966.

Printed in the United States of America
89 88 87   5 4 3 2

Library of Congress Cataloging in Publication Data

Built in the U.S.A.
    Bibliography: p.
    1. Architecture—United States.
I. Maddex, Diane.   II. Title: Built in the U.S.A.
NA705.B76   1985   720′ .973   84-26473
ISBN 0-89133-118-2

"Skyscrapers," by Ada Louise Huxtable, is adapted from an article that appeared in *The New Criterion*, November 1982, which formed the basis of *The Tall Building Artistically Reconsidered: The Search for a Skyscraper Style*, by Ada Louise Huxtable, to be published in 1985 by Pantheon Books. Copyright © 1982 by Ada Louise Huxtable. Reprinted by permission of the author and Georges Borchardt, Inc.

Designed by Anne Masters
Edited by Gretchen Smith, Associate Editor, The Preservation Press
Composed in Trump Mediaeval by Carver Photocomposition, Inc., Arlington, Va., and printed on 70# Frostbrite by Science Press, Ephrata, Pa.

Preface

If most people were asked to recall a famous architectural quotation, it is a safe bet that the majority would respond, "Form follows function." This maxim—expressed in 1896 by architect Louis Sullivan as "form ever follows function"—has been the subject of architectural debate ever since. Philip Johnson has asserted that "form follows form, not function." Frank Lloyd Wright insisted that "form and function are one." And Mies van der Rohe told us that "form, by itself, does not exist."

But whether form and function are separate, sequential or sometimes ephemeral, it seems inarguable that the function of most buildings can be deduced from the forms that have evolved for them over the years. A barn looks like a barn and not a bank—because its form responds to the function it must fill or because its builder replicated the traditional idea of "barn." In either case, looking at buildings from the viewpoint of their function is an important but often neglected way to understand American architecture.

Built in the U.S.A. examines the relationship between form and function in more than three dozen of our most pervasive building types. Our first book in this series, *What Style Is It? A Guide to American Architecture,* looks at buildings in terms of their architectural styles. A style can be adopted and applied to almost any building type, from Gothic Revival barns to Greek Revival outhouses. But studying buildings for the function they were meant to perform provides insights into an even larger spectrum of structures, especially those that do not exhibit any formal architectural style.

From airports to zoos, *Built in the U.S.A.* not only answers the question, What type of building is that? It also shows why a school looks like a school, a fort looks like a fort, a diner looks like a diner. And in the process, it creates a unique perspective on American architecture—and the age-old question of whether the form or the function came first.

Diane Maddex, Editor

■■■■■■■■■■■■■■■■■■■■■■■■■■■■■■■■■

AIRPORTS
Martin Greif

The airport is an ever-changing form, defying permanence. No airport ever built has been considered finished or complete or even up to date. The architecture of airport buildings is dependent on developments in aircraft technology: The design of the airplane determines the design of the airport, and not the other way around.

Contrary to popular usage of the term, an airport is not a building per se but the place on which a passenger terminal and other auxiliary structures stand; it is a place provided for the landing and takeoff of aircraft, usually also providing refueling, storage and other facilities. Early airports, brought into being as the first aircraft flights were made in the early 1900s, consisted of wooden ramps and cleared downhill runways that gave a smooth surface for takeoff.

When flying emerged from the purely experimental stages about 1910, the relatively small size of the aircraft then in use, coupled with their slow takeoff and landing speeds, made almost any open and level area a potential landing field. Consequently, the first airports were remarkably casual affairs—a canvas or frame hangar was almost all that was required. Until at least the 1920s, accommodations for passengers were negligible—hardly more than a chair or two in the manager's office in the hangar. Many early airports were more concerned with providing space for spectators, thrilled by the adventure of flight, than for passengers; in the 1920s and 1930s, many landing fields featured grandstands and even adjacent amusement parks and swimming pools for spectators.

The trend of aircraft design from small airplanes to the larger fast transports of the late 1930s brought about the birth of the modern airport. As aircraft grew larger and safer, airports were forced to follow suit. Runways became increasingly longer, and the buildings designed to house cargo, safety and maintenance facilities and the rapidly growing number of commercial passengers became larger and more sophisticated to handle ticketing, baggage retrieval, restaurant facilities, sewage systems, fire-fighting equipment and radar and electronic controls.

The commercial jetliner in the late 1950s transformed the whole facade and function of jet-age airports, resulting

College Park Airport (1909), College Park, Md., the world's oldest continually operating airport. Wilbur Wright instructed the first flying officers of the U.S. Army Signal Corps here. (U.S. Army)

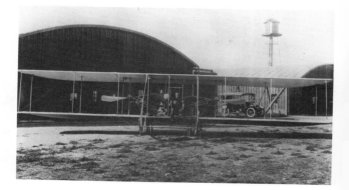

The Boeing Company's Red Barn (1909–10, E. W. Heath), Seattle, constructed soon after the company was contracted by the Army Air Corps to build training planes. (Boeing Company Archives)

in a worldwide building boom to adapt or completely rebuild them. In addition to building the enormous runways required for jet takeoffs and landings, airports throughout the 1960s changed their profiles by the addition of covered corridors telescoping out from the main terminal building to meet the planes. To get passengers to these satellite areas, some airports installed moving sidewalks and some completely eliminated passageways reaching out into the apron by moving passengers to the jets aboard giant "mobile lounges." Airport planners also installed revolving baggage carousels or perpetual motion conveyor belts to sort and store passengers' luggage automatically.

All this and far more—enormous parking lots, new highways, the development of the swinging, telescoping, covered aerogangplank—has hardly been enough, however, to counter airport planners' major problem: Airports have run out of space. Given the estimated number of people who will be using American airports in 10 years—one billion—how could any airport, new or old, be anything but overcrowded and obsolete even before it was built? It is doubtful that there is any massive architectural form more temporary than the modern airport. ★

Hangar No. 1 (1929), Los Angeles Municipal Airport, a Spanish colonial building that was actually two separate hangars connected by an administrative building. (Henry E. Huntington Library and Art Gallery)

Pan American Airways System Terminal Building (1933–34, Delano and Aldrich), Miami, with hangars in the background. The Streamline Moderne style was considered perfect for structures relating to high-speed travel. (Pan American World Airways)

Waiting room, Universal Air Lines passenger station (late 1920s), Chicago Municipal Airport (later Midway). (Missouri Historical Society)

Marine Air Terminal (c. 1940, William Adams Delano), La Guardia Airport, New York City, built to serve seaplanes. (David Sharpe, HAER)

Washington Dulles International Airport (1962, Eero Saarinen), Chantilly, Va., epitomizing the new age of flight. (Balthazar Korab)

Newark (N.J.) International Airport terminals (1973), branching out to satellite aircraft gate buildings, each with an upper departure level, a lower arrival level and a ground parking level. (Port Authority of New York and New Jersey)

AMUSEMENT PARKS AND FAIRS
Frederick and Mary Fried

Fairs are of ancient origin, beginning as trade and barter events, often celebrating some common holiday. Shelters were light and portable, and diversions were provided by acrobats, jugglers and primitive rides such as swings and carousels. England's St. Bartholomew Fair began in the 14th century and lasted into the mid-19th.

In America the tradition survived with state and county fairs, where durable structures for spectators and stock were erected in the Gothic Revival style made popular by Alexander Jackson Davis. After the Civil War, picnic grounds and family parks with carousels, boat rides and coasters were established. The architecture aped styles then in favor.

The first American world's fair was held in 1853 in the New York Crystal Palace, an iron and glass structure inspired by the 1851 greenhouse-style London Crystal Palace. The 1876 Philadelphia centennial influenced many subsequent world's fairs with its huge elaborate structures housing agricultural, arts and science exhibits and the industrial achievement of all nations.

Subsequent American world's fairs—Chicago in 1893, St. Louis in 1904 and San Francisco in 1915—were also designed by America's leading architects; many were trained in the Beaux-Arts tradition, which was reflected in the majestic buildings and their monumental sculpture. The buildings' function was to amaze the beholder with their exterior magnificence and splendor and to provide maximum exhibition space; only a few were permanent buildings. By the 1930s the baroque false fronts of the exhibition halls had given way to unadorned functionalism. The Trylon and Perisphere were symbols of New York's 1939–40 world's fair, whose theme was "The World of Tomorrow." The fair was dealt a severe setback by the outbreak of World War II, and recent fairs have faced serious problems of space and money.

Court of Honor (1893, C. B. Atwood, D. H. Burnham, F. L. Olmsted), World's Columbian Exposition, Chicago, which helped usher in an era of classical revival architecture. (Chicago Historical Society)

The Ferris wheel on the Plaisance (1893, George W. G. Ferris), Chicago, surrounded by minarets. (Frederick Fried Archives)

   Although the 1876 centennial provided no space for amusements, later fairs all included an amusement area. The skyline of Chicago's 1893 World's Columbian Exposition was dominated by the giant Ferris wheel.

   In 1903 Frederick W. Thompson created Luna Park at Coney Island, its turrets, towers and landscaped elevated promenades outlined by dazzling electric lights. In 1904 Dreamland Park, designed by architects Kirby, Pettit and Green, opened across the street. It was a mass of plaster fantasies defying description and style. Together with George C. Tilyou's Steeplechase Park, which had opened in 1897 a few blocks west, they formed the largest and most glittering amusement area in the world.

   With the depression, many old amusement parks were forced to shut down. A new type of park came into being with the opening of Disneyland in 1955. Its pseudo-historical constructions, fairy-tale castle and familiar cartoon characters appealed to Americans looking for safe, wholesome fun with overtones of educational value. Other corporation-owned theme parks followed.

   Today, few of the old amusement parks or their buildings remain. Dreamland and Luna Park burned in 1911; Luna, reconstructed, burned again in 1946. Steeplechase was torn down in 1966. At Sandusky, Ohio, Cedar Point is a modern park with several turn-of-the-century buildings unchanged and still in use. Charles Looff's 1916 Pleasure Pier and carousel building at Santa Monica, Calif., have withstood time and tide, minus a few domes. ★

Carousel building (1904, Horace Trumbauer), Pabst Park, Milwaukee. (Frederick Fried Archives)

Roller coaster (1910, LaMarcus A. Thompson), Venice, Calif. (Frederick Fried Archives)

Luna Park (1903, Frederick W. Thompson), Coney Island, N.Y. Its brilliant lights turned night into day and gave rise to the term "White City." (Frederick Fried Archives)

Carousel horse (c. 1912, Marcus Charles Illions), Brooklyn, N.Y. (Frederick Fried Archives)

Carousel (1922, William H. Dentzel), Glen Echo Park, Md., with hand-carved horses, figures and chariots. (Frederick Fried Archives)

Carousel building (1976, Randall Duell Associates), Marriott's Great America, Santa Clara, Calif. (Frederick Fried Archives)

Geodesic dome (1967, R. Buckminster Fuller), American Pavilion, Expo '67, Montreal, Canada. (Chris Lund, National Film Board of Canada)

APARTMENT BUILDINGS
John Hancock

The apartment building is a historically recent multiunit housing type. Its form originated with the so-called French flat in mid-19th-century Paris and spread quickly elsewhere during the Industrial Revolution as a means of housing large numbers of people closely, comfortably and profitably on increasingly valuable urban land. The prototype apartment house in the United States was the Stuyvesant (1869) in New York City, designed and built by architect Richard Morris Hunt. Since then, apartments have been built in a great variety of styles for every socioeconomic group in the nation.

An American apartment house usually has three or more stories and at least five (usually more than 10) separate households, all having a common street entrance and roof. From the 1870s on, palatial apartment houses for the very rich were built in prestigious downtown residential sections of most major cities. Typically, they had one tenant per floor (or two floors), more than a dozen rooms per unit and, until the 1920s, quarters for live-in servants. The ground and second floors were rented for professional offices, exclusive shops and restaurants because tenants would not live close to street level.

Luxury apartment houses for the affluent upper-middle class also became popular from the 1870s on. Architect-designed in every fashionable style, they were generally smaller than their palatial contemporaries, but the buildings were usually taller, the rooms fewer per unit, the tenant groups and interior arrangements more varied and the locations sometimes suburban.

By far the largest number of buildings, particularly between 1880 and 1930, are efficiency apartment houses for middle- and moderate-income groups. Most are three-to five-story walk-ups containing a variety of one- to five-room units, covering half a block or less and located near intersecting arterials, commercial subcenters or other multiunit dwellings or on the edge of neighborhoods of middle-income detached housing.

Since the 1950s many large projects have been built with urban renewal funds. Federally funded public housing apartment houses for low-income and, later, poor people have been built in most large cities since about 1934, at first mainly as two- to three-story garden apartments but often in the 1950s and 1960s as 20- to 30-story towers. These high-rises have not proved attractive to their residents or neighbors and are unfashionable in public housing today except in buildings for the elderly.

Regional variations are reflected in building materials, styles and number of users. However, middle-income and smaller apartments tend to have a plain, boxy look with flat roofs and little landscaping. But American apartments have been notable for well-equipped kitchens, good bathrooms and safe heating systems and for being cheaper rentals than detached houses.

American architectural studies rarely mention the apartment building, or they treat it as distinctly inferior housing. Nevertheless, most Americans have been or will be apartment dwellers at some stage in their lives, and this building type has become increasingly important in American architecture. ★

The Stuyvesant (1869, Richard Morris Hunt), New York City. (Charles von Urban, Museum of the City of New York)

Breakfast room, 1107 Fifth Avenue (1925, W. L. Rouse and L. A. Goldstone), New York City. (J. C. Maugans, courtesy Harmon H. Goldstone)

The Dakota (1884, Henry Janeway Hardenburgh), New York City, where the affluent still live. (HABS)

Marshall Field Garden Apartments (1929–30, Andrew J. Thomas and Ernest R. Graham), Chicago, the largest moderate-income housing development in the country before the depression. (Devereux Bowly, Jr.)

Parkchester (1929), Bronx, N.Y., a series of 12-story buildings on 130 acres housing 12,000 residents. (© The Bronx County Historical Society)

Pruitt-Igoe (1965, Minoru Yamasaki), St. Louis, a public housing project that became a notorious urban battleground and was razed in 1976. (HUD)

Lockefield Gardens (1936), Indianapolis, one of the country's first large-scale housing projects. (Robert Lavelle)

Marina City (1964–67, Bertrand
Goldberg Associates), Chicago,
two 62-story circular towers that
are virtual microcities.
(Hedrich-Blessing)

860–80 Lake Shore Drive
Apartments (1952, Ludwig Mies
van der Rohe), Chicago, steel
frame buildings in the
International Style. (Hedrich-
Blessing)

Guild House (1960–63, Venturi
and Rauch; Cope and Lippincott),
Philadelphia, Friends' housing for
the elderly. (Mark Cohn)

BANKS
S. Allen Chambers, Jr.

In 1818 the Newport (R.I.) *Mercury* announced the opening of a bank by asserting that "its extraordinary strength and solidity as a place of deposit, will essentially promote the designs of the Institution." A hundred years later, the November 1919 issue of *Architectural Record* praised a new bank that conveyed "in its appearance an impression that it reflects the character of the institution by its air of stability, dignity, and security." Obviously, the concept of what a bank should look like had not changed much over the years. Although banks early adopted the canons of classical architecture as appropriate forms to house their functions, the less tangible attributes of strength, security and stability characterize them as a distinguishable building type.

England had not allowed banks in its colonies, and the first American bank of truly national scope, the United States Bank in Philadelphia, was not established until 1791. When its headquarters was opened in 1797, the press lauded it as "the first finished building of any consequence, wherein true taste and knowledge has been displayed in this country." An architectural competition for the Second Bank of the United States in 1818 was won by William Strickland, who produced America's first public building to be modeled after the most familiar of classical monuments, the Parthenon. The transformation of the ancient temple to a temple of finance was now complete.

Templelike inside as well, banks almost invariably contain a large space, or banking room, that fully measures up to the expectations of the exterior. While floors are necessarily interrupted by desks, tellers' cages and counters, walls and ceilings are generally highly decorated. Vaults are usually featured attractions.

From 1870 to 1920, the number of banks increased from some 3,000 to more than 30,000. Although banks occasionally sought new architectural expression, the traditional visual virtues of strength and security were retained. The typical classical revival banks of this period

Opposite: First Bank of the United States (1795–97, Samuel Blodgett, Jr.), Philadelphia, the prototype of U.S. financial institutions. (Library of Congress)

Above: Second Bank of the United States (1818–24, William Strickland), Philadelphia, the first public building in America designed in imitation of the Parthenon. (Jack E. Boucher, HABS)

infuriated Louis Sullivan, who suggested that a banker might "wear a toga, sandals, and conduct his business in the venerated Latin tongue." Sullivan and other Prairie School practitioners designed a group of midwestern banks from 1906 to about 1918 that are among the most distinguished and indigenous products of American architecture. This period also witnessed the rise of the skyscraper bank, a product of both mergers and increased volumes of business. The typical skyscraper concept of a base, shaft and capital ensured that the main banking premises on the first floors could still be clothed in classical garb.

The creation in 1913 of the Federal Reserve System, which all national banks were required to join, had an immense effect on bank architecture. While the Federal Reserve banks became "bankers' banks" (and continued the traditional approach to bank design), the individual national banks began to appear less formidable and more inviting to potential customers. Also, branch banks were authorized.

By the 1950s, banks joined the migration to suburban shopping malls, adding drive-in windows for streamlined banking and sometimes threatening the existence of older downtown facilities. Home offices have had to devote more space to office use, and the newest Federal Reserve banks are essentially office towers. To their credit, banks were among the first institutions to become involved in the revitalization of downtowns in the 1960s and 1970s.

Still, the classically inspired designs say "bank" as nothing else. When a bank in the District of Columbia was converted to a retail store, its architectural identity was so strong that the new owners felt compelled to post a sign announcing, "This is not a bank." They were wrong—architecturally, it still is and always will be. ★

Conjectural drawing of the interior of a bank, c. 1900. The floor space is divided into tellers' cages and counters, but the ornate coffered ceiling gives the room visual unity. (Frye and Chesterman)

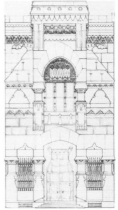

Provident Life and Trust Company (1876–79, Frank Furness), Philadelphia, reflecting the High Victorian Gothic style. (Dellas H. Harder, HABS)

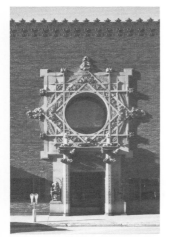

First National Bank (1885), Hampton, Va., a Romanesque building occupying a prominent location. (Cheyne's Studio, Symes Eaton Museum)

Merchants' National Bank (Poweshiek County National Bank) (1914, Louis Sullivan), Grinnell, Iowa. Although Prairie Style characteristics are evident, the rose window in its exuberant terra-cotta surround is unique. (Robert Thall, HABS)

Philadelphia Savings Fund Society (1931–32, George Howe and William Lescaze), Philadelphia. This monument of modern architecture contains shops on the street level, a banking room on the second floor and an office tower above. (D. E. Sutton)

BARNS
Thomas C. Hubka

All European settlers brought barn building traditions to the New World, but the English and German traditions had the most significant impact on the development of the American barn. The standard English barn was a wooden, gabled structure with doors in the middle of the side wall and was initially used for grain threshing and storage; however, the severity of winters in the New World necessitated the inclusion of livestock and hay. The German tradition of large, centralized barn construction was developed into a type known today as the Pennsylvania barn, a two-level structure with an overhanging forebay; livestock were housed on the ground level and hay and grain stored on the second floor.

Despite regional diversity, American barn development has fluctuated between centralized, single barns and diversified, multiple barns. During the late 1700s and early 1800s, many eastern farmers abandoned the European multiple barn tradition in favor of a centralized barn as used by the Germans and Dutch to shelter many types of activities. By the end of the 19th century and continuing into the 20th century, the centralized barn began to be replaced by specialized barns housing separate activities resulting from specialization and greater volume of agricultural production. Beginning about 1880–1900, exterior silos were developed and used increasingly for converting grain to livestock feed. Many southern farmers, maintaining a multiple barn tradition, have used barns to shelter crops and provided only minimal shelter for their animals.

In the 19th century, Americanized versions of the English and German traditions were transported into the Midwest and the West and were combined into two basic types of barns: the general purpose or feeder barn, used primarily for crops but also for farm vehicles and general storage, and a two-story basement or dairy barn, which housed cattle on the ground floor and hay on the second floor. These two basic types exist in various regional forms in many areas of the country and are perhaps the most common types of barns in America today.

English, Dutch, German and Scandinavian barn builders brought complex medieval systems of heavy timber, mortise-and-tenon framing and log construction.

English-style stone barn at Linden (late 1700s), the estate of Lord Baltimore's brother-in-law, Baltimore County, Md. (E. H. Pickering, HABS)

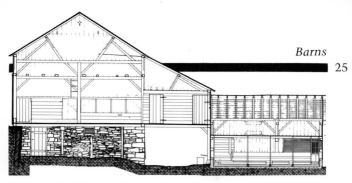

Kautz Barn (c. 1877), near Shawnee, Pa., a product of the area's long tradition of Germanic folk architecture. (William H. Edwards, HABS)

American builders gradually simplified many aspects of these systems that proved impractical, including roof thatching, brick wall infilling or nogging, stacked logs and the practice of living in, or close to, the barn. In older European-influenced forms, the major barn door was usually located in the side, under the eave. Beginning in the 1800s, American builders developed barns with doors located in the gable ends. The three- and four-bay long barn plan is the most common.

Between 1820 and 1920 barn builders gradually changed the barn's basic structural framing to the modern, lightweight balloon frame and nail system. As a result, the double-sloped gambrel roof replaced the single-sloped gabled roof, the most common roof form until the late 19th century. Before 1940 most barn roofs were wood shingled. Floors in the North tend to be wood planking, while in the South earthen floors often are used; some barns have combination flooring.

The survival of older wooden barns is being threatened by the increasing use of prefabricated barns with metal sheathing, wood truss frames and concrete floors. Many farmers have found the cost of maintaining huge wooden structures to be prohibitive, and they are either taken down or left to fall down. ★

Shaker round barn (1826), Hancock, Mass., with detail of wood roof supports. (Mitchell; Jack E. Boucher, HABS)

Gambrel-roof barn with Japanese-style painting by Douglas Tyler, near Lansing, Mich. (Balthazar Korab)

Barn complex with silos, outbuildings and rainbow-roof barn, near Clare, Mich. (Balthazar Korab)

Barn raising on the Rainy River around 1895, Minnesota. (Minnesota Historical Society)

Joseph Conrad Farm (Miller's Farm), near Mt. Pleasant, Pa., a German barn with a gabled roof. (Perry Benson, HABS)

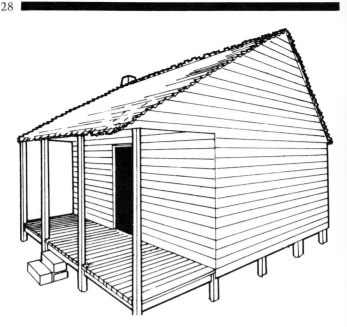

BLACK SETTLEMENTS
Everett L. and La Barbara Wigfall Fly

The form and structure of black settlements in the
United States, first accurately recorded in the 18th
century, were limited by colonial traditions of slavery and
racial separatism and belief in ethnic superiority. More
than 800 black settlements, sharing many similarities,
have existed throughout the country. Black settlements
did not adhere to traditional Western designs or to African
building traditions, which were discouraged by whites. As
a result, black structures were vernacular in nature and
eclectic in style. Since the colonial era, seven basic
settlement types have evolved: the slave village, freedmen's village, rural village, black town, urban enclave,
rural resettlement community and alley dwelling.
    Slave villages on southern plantations used the most
basic architectural forms for sleeping and domestic
quarters. In most slave villages, blacks built their own
buildings but were not given the authority to design
them—i.e., determine the form, massing or materials—
although they did incorporate some of their traditional
building technology. Freedmen's villages, established in
the South by the federal government after Emancipation,
served as temporary communities for emancipated blacks
until the 1880s. Accommodations included tents, barracks
and abandoned slave cabins. Following Emancipation,
rural villages also were established in the South, many on
abandoned lands. Groups or families were often deeded
tracts of land by whites, and in some regions blacks
banded together and pooled their resources to purchase
tracts. These rural villages often evolved into black towns
by the late 1880s and survived through World War II.
Black towns throughout the country represented the peak
of independent physical and social community development. Black enclaves, which developed in northern cities
before 1865 and in other regions following Emancipation,
displayed the most sophisticated community forms,
including housing, commercial structures, churches,

Opposite: A typical slave cabin made of wood with a steeply pitched roof creating a sleeping loft. (National Archives)

Below: Uncle Sam Plantation (early 1800s), Convent, La., with slave cabins several miles from the main house. (Joseph P. Marlow, HABS)

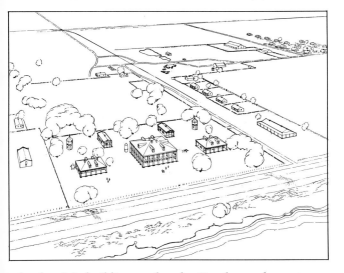

schools, civic buildings and parks. Rural resettlement communities were planned communities in the southeastern United States, intended to assist farmers devastated by the natural disasters of the 1930s. Alley dwellings developed as housing for central-city black domestics, day laborers and their families. Between 1876 and 1950, blacks lived in shacks and carriage houses in alleys and interior courts, hidden by large, elegant houses that faced the street.

The architecture of the earliest settlement types was simple. The one-story frame or stone vernacular house dominated these communities. The more structured communities—rural villages and black towns—frequently developed around a small group of public buildings that included a church, school and lodge hall. All were built by contractors or local residents.

By contrast, the architecture of urban black enclaves was frequently complex, multistory masonry construction based on a classical style and designed by a black master builder or black architect. Despite the disappearance of black enclaves, large structures such as Antioch Baptist Church (1891) in Houston, Tex., and Booker T. Washington High School (1926) in Miami, Fla., remain landmarks amid urban growth. Restrictions on black education limited the number of trained black architects until the late 19th century. By 1900 design professionals were trained at small black vocational and industrial schools in the South.

Many of the urban black enclaves were destroyed or significantly altered by 1960s urban renewal programs and later revitalization projects. Black settlements such as Robbins, Ill., Nicodemus, Kans., East St. Louis, Ill., and Kendleton, Tex., are still identifiable, but less than 10 percent are listed in the National Register of Historic Places, in part because of fragmentation of data, these communities' financial inability to support restoration projects and lack of understanding of the historical value of black sites. ★

African House (c. 1820), Melrose, La., part of Melrose Plantation, which was established by free blacks. (Paul Thebideaux)

Site plan of Freedmen's Village (1863), Arlington Heights, Va., established by the federal government for emancipated southern slaves. (National Archives)

Black school (1917), District No. 1, Nicodemus, Kans., a town established in the 1870s by blacks migrating from rural southern and border state areas. (Clay Fraser, HABS)

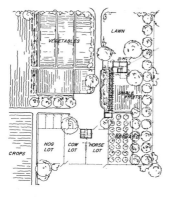

Farm layout proposed by the Rural Resettlement Administration, created in 1935 to assist low-income farmers, including many blacks. (National Archives)

Black houses (1890–1935), Fourth
Ward, now the Freedmen's Town Historic District, Houston, characterized
by one- and two-story frame buildings, including duplexes and shotgun
houses, set close to narrow streets.
(Texas Historical Commission)

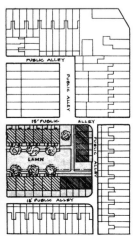

"Jockey Ring" (c. 1900), a block in
the black enclave of East St. Louis,
Ill. (Illinois State Historical Library)

Plot plan of Hopkins Place,
Washington, D.C., a proposal for
rehabilitating this area of alley
dwellings. (National Archives)

BREWERIES
Dianne Newell

The brewing industry has furnished some of the most distinctive and unusual industrial architecture in the Western world. In North America, the first commercial brewery was erected in the New Netherlands in 1612; by 1800 breweries were to be found throughout the northeastern United States.

The function of the brewhouse—essentially a big kitchen—led to its particular construction and arrangement. The two most dominant operations were the frequent raising and lowering of liquid temperatures and the handling and storing of liquids and solids. Until the 1870s, when steam heating and artificial refrigeration were introduced, breweries were small-scale enterprises. Brewing was a hand operation, based on gravity flow and limited to winter months, when the air reached temperatures suitable for cooling. Breweries served local markets because beer would neither travel well nor endure long periods without refrigeration. Albany, Brooklyn, Philadelphia and Baltimore were the brewing centers.

The early brewhouses were relatively plain, one- or two-story buildings with a tower, to the top of which water and malt were hoisted for boiling, and cellars often of two or more levels for cold storage of beer and ice. Windows had to be tiny and few in number in order to admit a small amount of light but no heat. Ventilation was supplied by special devices such as shutter flaps, louvers in the upper stories and roof ventilators. Roofs normally were gabled and covered with wooden shingles to resist heat; their profiles were broken by a chimney and cupolas or ventilators. A brewery complex might include a stable, cooperage, blacksmith's shop, bottling works, storage shed, workers' housing and an owner's dwelling.

Although the basic brewing technology remained unchanged, the beer market and brewing technology and, consequently, brewhouse architecture underwent considerable change after 1870. With expanded markets, large-batch processing and more efficient transportation, beer making fast became a year-round operation no longer restricted to northern locations. Steam heat and artificial refrigeration adjusted temperatures, and mechanical power (steam and, by the 1890s, electricity) was used to run the refrigeration compressors and other machinery. Midwestern cities, such as Cincinnati and Milwaukee, became major new brewing centers.

By 1880 the brewhouse was an enormous multistory structure of massive fireproof, factory construction. Because temperatures were mechanically regulated, many windows were feasible. The brewery complex expanded to include an office building, a power plant and maltings, which were highly functional structures made up of a series of low-clearance stories with numerous tiny, closely spaced window openings and paved floors on which germinating grain was spread, as well as a kiln for drying.

The brewhouses built after 1860 continued to display the characteristics of functional design, but their exteriors also reflected the eclectic High Victorian architectural style of the day. Furthermore, the breweries of the Northeast and Midwest frequently were expressions of the

American Brewery (Weissner Brewery) (1884–87), Baltimore, Md. This view shows the ventilators needed for the boiling process. (Wm. Edmund Barrett, HAER)

Lone Star Brewing Company (1895–1904, E. Jungerfeld and Company), San Antonio, now the home of the San Antonio Museum of Art. (NTHP Collection)

German origins of their owners and workers. An outstanding example is the American Brewery (1884–87) in Baltimore, whose style has been variously described as "Middle-European Chalet" or "Germanesque-Teutonic Pagoda." Usually, breweries were designed by a specialized architectural firm, such as Terney's of New York.

Several dozen historic brewhouses still stand in good repair but most of them are abandoned and unprotected. Because they are so specialized, so large and located in run-down districts, they have been neglected by community leaders and planners. Recently, however, imaginative plans have been made to adapt historic brewhouses in Albany, Baltimore, Honolulu, San Antonio and Denver for use as cultural centers. ★

Tivoli-Union Brewery (Milwaukee Brewery) (1890–91), Denver, one of the last gravity-fed breweries in the United States, now being converted to retail use. (Wm. Edmund Barrett, HAER)

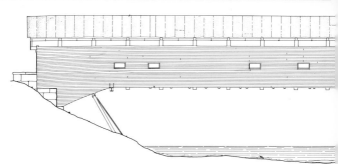

BRIDGES
Donald C. Jackson

An amazing variety of structural forms has been designed to carry human commerce over natural barriers. The type of bridge selected for a crossing depends on many factors, including geologic and topographic conditions at the site, the nature of traffic intended to use the span, the skills and availability of local workers, the price and availability of structural materials, the political influence of local suppliers and contractors and the visual prominence of the setting. Even within stable communities, wide variation in bridge types can exist.

American bridge building began in the colonial era, but almost none of the wooden and masonry bridges built in America before 1800 survives. Numerous 19th-century stone arch bridges, however, still stand in the eastern half of the United States. The tradition of masonry bridge construction continued until the turn of the 20th century in many regions, but by the middle of the 19th century stone arch bridges were rapidly being eclipsed by more readily built wood and metal structures.

Covered wooden truss bridges were built throughout the 19th century; starting in the 1840s, combination wood and iron trusses, and later all-metal trusses, began to supplant them in popularity. Today, several hundred covered bridges still stand, with most dating from the post–Civil War era. Other major types of early 19th-century highway spans include iron suspension bridges and wooden arch bridges. Although much less common than wooden trusses, these types were often used for particularly wide crossings.

By the middle of the 19th century, America's burgeoning railroad and highway systems required the construction of many new bridges. To meet this demand, the all-metal truss gradually developed into a popular form of American bridge during the late 19th and early 20th centuries. It was built in patented forms such as the Pratt, Warren and Bollman trusses, often by companies specializing in bridge fabrication. Other types of steel bridges built during this period often resembled truss bridges but, because of specific design features, were structurally different. These include a variety of movable bridges and certain types of cantilever or continuous spans. The long-span steel arch found use at many crossings; however, for the longest spans, the modern suspension bridge continues to reign as the most economically feasible to build. For short-span bridges the steel girder has found wide usage and is still used extensively on many highways.

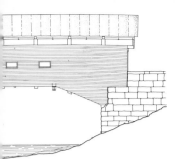

Covered bridge (1853), Barrackville,
W. Va. (Frederick R. Love, HAER)

Columbia and Nehaleon Railroad trestle, Kerry, Ore. Wood was commonly used for early trestle and covered bridges because of its wide availability. (Oregon Historical Society)

Small reinforced concrete bridges began appearing in the 1890s, and during the early 20th century they were built in profusion. Although a reinforced concrete bridge was usually more expensive to construct than a comparable steel truss bridge, local authorities were attracted to this type of bridge because initial maintenance costs were lower and locally produced materials could be used in construction. For short spans the reinforced concrete girder found some favor, but most reinforced concrete bridges are arched. The most common types are the deck arch, in which the roadway is carried above the structure's arch, and the rainbow arch, in which the roadway is suspended from arches extending above the deck.

During the past 15 years the Federal Highway Administration has administered programs designed to replace old and obsolete bridges in America's highway system and is scheduled to remove more than 250,000 "unsafe" bridges from service during the next several years. Many of these spans are historically significant, but, unfortunately, most will be totally replaced by new structures. As demonstrated by numerous historic bridge inventories, very few 19th-century highway bridges are still in operation. Although several local preservation groups have been successful in efforts to save historic bridges, the vast majority of historic bridges in America will not survive until the 21st century unless there is a dramatic, and unforeseen, change in public transportation policy. ★

State Street Bridge (c. 1900), Chicago, one of the first rolling-lift bascule bridges. (Chicago Historical Society)

Golden Gate Bridge (1933–37, J. B. Strauss), San Francisco, one of the most well-known suspension bridges in the world. (Carleton Knight III, NTHP)

Brooklyn Bridge (1869–83, John and Washington Roebling), New York City, the longest suspension bridge in the world when built. (Jet Lowe, HAER)

Bellows Falls Arch Bridge (1905, 1936), Bellows Falls, Vt., once the longest single-span highway bridge in the United States. (Jet Lowe, HAER)

Smithfield Street Bridge (1883, 1891, Gustav Lindenthal), Pittsburgh, a lenticular metal truss bridge. (Jack E. Boucher, HAER)

Eads Bridge (1869–74, James Buchanon Eads), St. Louis. The triple-span, tubular metallic arch construction was considered a radical design. (Jet Lowe, HAER)

A two-story, two-aisle lattice truss covered bridge (c. 1876, E. T. Fairbanks and Company), St. Johnsbury, Vt. (Eric DeLony, HAER)

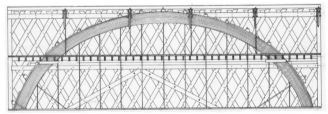

Georgia-Carolina Memorial Bridge (1927), an 11-span, reinforced concrete, open spandrel arch bridge. (Dennis O'Kain, HAER)

Cape Cod Canal Bridge (1935), Buzzards Bay, Mass., the longest vertical-lift bridge in the world when built. (David Plowden)

CAPITOLS
William Seale

The state capitol, like the skyscraper, is uniquely American. Born with the rise of American democracy, the form is today recognized all over the world as the appropriate architecture for democratic legislatures. The United States Capitol (1793–1867, William Thornton; Benjamin H. Latrobe; Charles Bulfinch; Thomas U. Walter) is a classic example of the type, although by the time its first phase was completed in 1821, some state capitols had long before adopted the "capitol" image.

The capitol form consists of a vertical element (usually but not necessarily a dome), balanced wings, a decorative frontispiece (usually a portico) and a great central space within, such as a rotunda, between balanced houses of legislature. "Style" is not a determining factor, although the classical is predominant. The elements of the state capitol form appeared separately during the colonial period as additions made by the assemblies to existing statehouses; for example, a great steeple built in the 1750s gave the Pennsylvania statehouse (1739–48, Andrew Hamilton and Edmund Woolley) a dramatic vertical thrust; the Virginia capitol (1699–1703, attributed to Gov. Francis Nicholson) in Williamsburg, after being wholly destroyed by fire, was reconstructed in the early 1750s with a bold new portico. These architectural features were united in 1810 in one building, the Pennsylvania State Capitol (1810–21, Stephen Hills), marking the full development of the capitol form. All capitols thereafter incorporated these architectural symbols of democracy.

Of the existing state capitols, only four survive from the 18th century: Maryland (1772–79, Joseph Horatio Anderson), Virginia (1785–98, Thomas Jefferson), New Jersey (1789–92, attributed to Jonathan Doan) and Massachusetts (1795–98, Charles Bulfinch). The capitols of Virginia and Massachusetts reflect intellectual opinions on how an American capitol should be; Virginia's is an imitation of an ancient Roman temple, and Massachusetts's is a simplified version of the British government structure Somerset House. The Massachusetts statehouse spawned many of similar plan in New England. A powerful influence in the South came from the remodeling (1818–21) of the now-vanished North Carolina statehouse (1792–94, Redham Adkins) into a full-fledged capitol like Pennsylvania's, with a dome, portico, rotunda and balanced legislative houses.

The Greek Revival style fit the form well. Far and above the finest is the old Kentucky capitol (1829–30, Gideon Shryock). Usually rectangular, most of the Greek Revival capitols had porticoes on the side—not temple style, on the end—with a central dome or domed lantern

Opposite: Virginia State Capitol
(1699–1703, attributed to Francis
Nicholson), Williamsburg. (Bodleian
Library, Oxford; Colonial Williamsburg Foundation)

Virginia State Capitol (1785–98,
Thomas Jefferson), Richmond, the
first adaptation of a Roman temple
to a complex modern purpose.
(Virginia State Travel Service)

Massachusetts Statehouse
(1795–98, Charles Bulfinch; 1831,
1856, 1895–98, 1914, 1917), Boston,
as it appeared in 1900, before the
addition of the wings. (Society for
the Preservation of New England
Antiquities)

Pennsylvania Old State Capitol
(1810–21, Stephen Hills), Har-
risburg. (Analectic Magazine, July
1820)

North Carolina Capitol (1832–40, Ithiel Town and A. J. Davis), Raleigh, an adaptation of the Parthenon model to a cruciform plan. (North Carolina Division of Archives and History)

United States Capitol (1793–1867, William Thornton, B. H. Latrobe, Charles Bulfinch), Washington, D.C., as it appeared in 1847, before the wings and dome by Thomas U. Walter were added. (Library of Congress)

of relatively large scale, lighting an inner rotunda with balanced houses on each side. During the popularity of the Greek Revival, two capitols challenged the domination of the dome. Completed in 1860, the Ohio capitol (1838–60, Thomas Cole) and the Tennessee capitol (1845–60, William Strickland) reintroduced the steeple tower. Other towers were being planned but were stopped by the Civil War, at which time completion of the monumental cast-iron dome in Washington (1855–63, Thomas U. Walter) gave the dome renewed vigor as a symbol of the Union.

The remaining capitols fall into three categories: The first two, the Victorian eclectic (1860s to early 1890s) and the neoclassical (1893 to World War I), generally suggest the national capitol in Washington, while the third might be termed "vernacular" capitols. This last group, all 20th century, takes two forms: the skyscraper and abstract designs based on geographical or ethnic forms and symbols. Bertram Goodhue designed the first vernacular capitol for Nebraska in 1919, a striking tower building meant to reflect the native architecture of the western plains. Delaware scrapped a concrete skyscraper for a quaint capitol "village" inspired by the then-rising Colonial Williamsburg.

New Mexico's capitol (1965–66, W. C. Kruger) was inspired by the sun symbol of ancient Indians but is decorated with portals adapted from Territorial-style structures in Santa Fe's historic district. The last of the vernacular capitols stands in Honolulu (1965–69, Belt, Lemmon and Lo and John Carl Warnecke) near Iolani Palace. The newest capitol, it represents the natural growth of the islands as volcanoes from the sea, and it is designed to be seen first from the air. ★

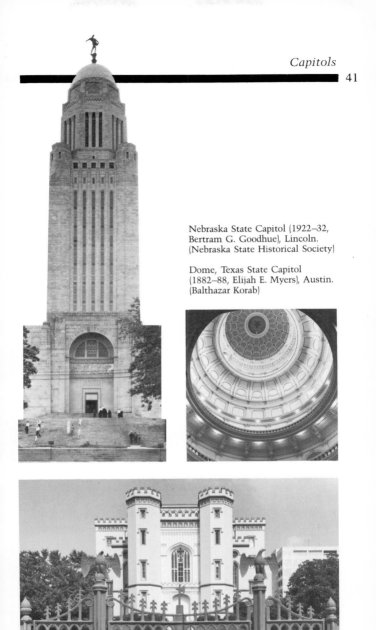

Nebraska State Capitol (1922–32, Bertram G. Goodhue), Lincoln. (Nebraska State Historical Society)

Dome, Texas State Capitol (1882–88, Elijah E. Myers), Austin. (Balthazar Korab)

Louisiana Old State Capitol (1847–49, James H. Dakin; reconstructed 1880–82, William A. Freret), Baton Rouge, one of only two antebellum Gothic capitols, a style seldom used for government buildings. (David J. Kaminsky, HABS)

New Mexico State Capitol (1965–66, W. C. Kruger), Sante Fe, designed in traditional Territorial style. (New Mexico Tourism and Travel Department)

CITY HALLS
William L. Lebovich

When Boston built its (and perhaps the colonies') first town hall in 1657, it had to satisfy certain functional and symbolic needs. The town hall provided a large public assembly room as well as administrative space, and its twin belfries represented the citizens' right to assembly. In the more than 300 years since Boston's town hall was built, American city halls have continued to evolve in response to changing functional and symbolic needs.

American municipal government has become increasingly specialized. During the colonial period, the same men wrote a town's laws, administered them and punished those who violated them. By the early 19th century, government had become sufficiently specialized to warrant separate legislative and judicial branches. By the mid-19th century, several local governments had become further specialized to have distinct police, fire, sanitation, water and health departments. But even these governments were not able to administer effectively the burgeoning, volatile 19th-century cities, and the power of the mayor was substantially increased. With the emergence of the strong mayor and, in the 20th century, the city manager, local government became further specialized; the legislative and administrative branches became clearly distinct units of government with different responsibilities and powers.

As municipal government became specialized into separate departments, more frequently these departments were housed separately from city hall. Unlike Boston's 17th-century town hall, which had room for all branches of government and the town market, a 20th-century city hall seldom houses more than the legislature (council), the mayor and a few administrative departments. The police and fire departments and the courts, to cite the most important agencies, have had their own, often grand, buildings since at least the late 19th century.

As the number of departments housed in the city hall has decreased, so has the grandeur of the interiors. Even a modest 18th-century city hall had an assembly hall, while many 19th-century city halls possessed magnificent multistory council chambers and courtrooms as well as impressive rotundas, atriums and grand staircases. All these spaces were public spaces, and as the city halls became mostly administrative offices, the public came into these buildings less often, thus creating less need for impressive public spaces.

Despite the decreased emphasis on the interiors, they as well as the exteriors continued to reflect changing American architectural styles. City halls in earlier periods were designed in popular styles such as classical revival or Gothic Revival, and late 19th-century city halls were frequently Richardsonian Romanesque buildings.

While the city hall interiors have become simpler, their exteriors have become more complex, more provocative. The increased emphasis on exteriors reflects the reality that the city hall's symbolic importance—expressed by its exteriors—has superseded its functional role—now simply to provide office space. The dramatic, inverted pyramid shape of Boston's current city hall, like many contemporary city halls, is intended to symbolize the city's rebirth. ★

Boston's 17th-century town hall (1657) and its present city hall (1963–69, Kallman, McKinnell and Knowles; Campbell, Aldrich and Nulty) near Faneuil Hall. (Charles A. Lawrence, The Bostonian Society; Ezra Stoller)

Wilmington Old Town Hall (1798–1800, John Way and Peter Brynberg), Wilmington, Del. This Federal-style city hall has the massing and silhouette common to municipal buildings of the late 18th century. (John Newell, Jr., HABS)

Brockton City Hall (1892–94, Wesley Lyng Minor), Brockton, Mass., reflecting a movement from the Richardsonian Romanesque to a more ornamental style. (Peter Vanderwarker, HABS)

Philadelphia City Hall (1871–1901, John McArthur, Jr., and Thomas U. Walter), an audacious example of Second Empire–style architecture. (Jack E. Boucher, HABS)

Council chamber, Charleston City Hall (1800–01, attributed to Gabriel Manigault), Charleston, S.C., a Federal-style structure originally built as a bank. (Charles Bayless, HABS)

Tooele City Hall (1867), Tooele, Utah, a simple but handsome red sandstone structure that also served as a courthouse. (Charles D. Harker, HABS)

Kansas City City Hall (1936–37, Wight and Wight), Kansas City, Mo., a stripped modern skyscraper with Art Deco ornamentation. (Paul Kivett, HABS)

Buffalo City Hall (1929–31, Dietel and Wade; Sullivan W. Jones), with WPA-era sculpture by Albert T. Stewart depicting Buffalo's industries. (John W. Cowper Company, Inc., HABS)

Dallas City Hall (1972–77, I. M. Pei and Partners; Harper and Kemp), a bold and monumental concrete trapezoidal building. (Frank Branger, HABS)

COLLEGES AND UNIVERSITIES
Thomas J. Schlereth

Beginning with Harvard College in 1636, the United
States has built more colleges and universities and
distributed them more widely than any other nation.
Although often begun as a single building—a revered Old
Main where students slept, ate, studied and had classes—
the building type is usually thought of as an aggregate of
several buildings often arranged with some degree of site
design. American colleges and universities usually share
several general characteristics: planning, residentiality and
tradition.

The idea of a campus as space enclosed or surrounded
by college structures is largely an American landscape
concept. Several designs have been influential: the three-
sided Cambridge quadrangle as originally proposed for
Harvard and William and Mary; the University of Virginia
concept of a colonnaded "academical village"—an open
lawn or green surrounded by modest living quarters;
Frederick Law Olmsted's picturesque suburban communities sited in informal parklike settings and favored by
various land-grant colleges; and the Beaux-Arts symmetry
of formal areas and central vistas as in the designs for
Stanford and the new campus at Columbia.

Until the instant urban campuses of the 20th century,
most American colleges and universities grew piecemeal.
Frequently Old Main was first the entire physical plant
and then the focal point of the campus as other structures
developed. Specialty buildings found on the American
campus include religious structures, libraries and laboratories. In the 20th century, athletic facilities—stadiums,
amphitheaters and sports complexes—became a standard
part of the collegiate environment.

Thomas Jefferson's University of Virginia plan articu-
lated the collegiate residential ideal for a large open space
surrounded by professors' houses serving also as class-
rooms and alternating with student rooms; its typical
expression was the student dormitory, probably the most
ubiquitous building type on the American campus. Other
solutions to the American penchant for on-campus living
have been Harvard's house system, Yale's residential
colleges and the rise of the fraternity and sorority house
system.

Colleges and universities built in the 19th century
reflect the diversity of architectural styles during that

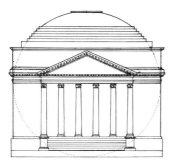

The lawn of the University of Virginia (1817–26, Thomas Jefferson), Charlottesville, designed to harmonize art and nature, with the Rotunda as the centerpiece. (Information Services, University of Virginia)

Harvard Yard, Harvard University (1636), Cambridge, Mass., with Daniel Chester French's sculpture of John Harvard and enclosed by late 18th- and early 19th-century dormitories. (Harvard University News Office)

period. Styles popular in the 20th century include Beaux-Arts, colonial revival (English and Spanish) and the English Gothic. "Collegiate Gothic," as interpreted by Ralph Adams Cram at Princeton or Henry Ives Cobb at the University of Chicago, featuring soaring towers, became a national substyle for higher education for a period early in this century.

Twentieth-century collegiate architecture, while much attached to the traditional styles, has also flirted with the Modern movement; various campuses (MIT, Yale, Harvard) contain many examples of the International Style. The 20th-century American university tends to be a complex urban form, a place possessing many of the building types—power plants, hotels, transportation networks, convention centers, parking lots and skyscrapers—that also characterize the modern American city. ★

Davenport College (1930, James Gamble Rogers), Yale University, New Haven, Conn., a Georgian-style residential dormitory. (Yale University)

Old Morrison (1833, Gideon Shryock), Transylvania University, Lexington, Ky., a Greek Revival design. (Transylvania University)

Gymnasium (1880, Peter J. Williamson), Vanderbilt University, Nashville, a Gothic Revival structure now used as the fine arts building. (William H. Edwards, HABS)

Stanford University (1887–91, Shepley, Rutan and Coolidge), Stanford, Calif., with buildings in the Spanish revival style. (News and Publications Service, Stanford University)

Chapel (1930–32, Horace Trumbauer), Duke University, Durham,
N.C., a Collegiate Gothic building
with a 210-foot tower. (Duke
University)

Annie Pfeiffer Chapel (1938, Frank
Lloyd Wright), Florida Southern
College, Lakeland, Fla., built of
concrete blocks designed by Wright.
(Brad Beck, Florida Southern College)

Kresge Auditorium (1956, Eero
Saarinen), Massachusetts Institute
of Technology, Cambridge, Mass.
(Calvin Campbell, MIT)

Crown Hall (1945–46, Ludwig
Mies van der Rohe), Illinois Institute of Technology, Chicago, a
classic example of the International Style. (Hedrich-Blessing)

COMMUNAL SOCIETIES
Donald E. Pitzer

Only a few of the thousands of communal groups in America have endured long enough to create notable buildings. These structures do not represent any single architectural style but are linked by their massive, sturdy, functional qualities. Their designs usually reflect the communalists' beliefs and lifestyles. Most were built with readily available materials and methods, and their structural forms usually are simple, sometimes innovative and often aesthetically pleasing.

The four-story Sisters' House and Chapel of the monastic Seventh-Day Baptists at Ephrata Cloister (1735–86) in Ephrata, Pa., are perhaps the best remaining examples of medieval German architecture in America. Surviving log and stone buildings at the Moravian Community (1744–62) at Bethlehem, Pa., include their 1742 Gemein Haus (Common House), thought to be the largest extant log structure in the United States, their four-story stone tannery (1761) and waterworks (1762).

The 19 Shaker settlements from New England to Kentucky (1787–present) have left a legacy of workshops, simple meetinghouses, giant barns and huge "family houses" that could accommodate 80 celibate members living in sexually segregated quarters. The round barn (1826) at Hancock, Mass., is remarkable. At Pleasant Hill, Ky., Micajah Burnett designed an ingenious trestle system to support the upper stories of the meetinghouse (1820) to permit the Shaker dances to proceed unobstructed by columns in the sanctuary below.

The German-American Harmony Society (1804–1916) built three towns: Harmony (1804–14) and Economy (1825–1916), now Ambridge, Pa., and New Harmony (1814–24), Ind. Preserved at Harmony and Economy are dwellings for celibate nuclear families and vaulted wine cellars; at Economy, the Feast Hall, which housed an adult school, printing press and dining room seating 500; at New Harmony, a granary and reconstructed hedge labyrinth. Harmonists who left Economy in the 1830s founded Bethel, Mo. (1844–80), and Aurora, Ore. (1856–81).

Opposite: Sisters'
House and Chapel
(1740–46), Ephrata
Cloister, Ephrata, Pa.
(Ephrata Cloister)

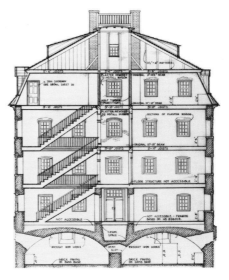

Single Brethren's
House (1748), Beth-
lehem, Pa. (Allan
Steenhusen, HABS)

The German Separatists of Zoar, Ohio (1817–98), have
left, among other structures, an unusual greenhouse and
the large mansion of leader Joseph Bimeler. Swedish
Bishop Hill, Ill. (1846–62), has preserved its Bjorklund
Hotel, Steeple Building, church, schoolhouse, store,
dairymaid's buildings, shops, hospital and founder Eric
Janson's house. Nearly all of the hundreds of original
frame, stone and brick structures built by the Amana
Society, German immigrants who lived communally in
seven villages in Iowa from 1855 to 1932, are still being
used by community descendants. Numerous Mormon
brick dwellings and shops, including the house of Brigham
Young, have been meticulously reconstructed from original plans in their communal Nauvoo, Ill. (1841–46), as
well as in Salt Lake City and other settlements in Utah,
where native stone was widely used; the temple at
Kirtland, Ohio, has also been reconstructed. Scores of
monasteries, convents, workshops and chapels have been
built by the Benedictine, Cistercian and Trappist Roman
Catholic orders throughout the United States since the
1840s. The austere buildings of about 50 Hutterite
colonies may be seen in the Dakotas and Montana.

Innovative buildings are associated with several communal groups. John Humphrey Noyes's perfectionist
followers, who practiced complex marriage, built an
enormous Mansion House in stages at Oneida, N.Y.
(1848–81). This complex, which housed more than 250
members and contained "social rooms" for love making,
is still occupied by community descendants. Katherine
Tingley's Theosophical Point Loma (1897–1940) at San
Diego, Calif., boasted two large buildings with aqua-
marine and amethyst domes and a Greek amphitheater
overlooking the Pacific. Geodesic domes and zomes
invented by R. Buckminster Fuller were adopted by many
youth communes in the 1960s and are still important
features of several communities. Perhaps the most
elaborate communal building in American history was
completed in 1979 by the New Vrindaban Hare Krishna
ashram near Limestone, W. Va. Prabhupada's Palace, an
ornate, oriental-style building, rises in the unlikely setting
of rolling farmland. ★

Top: Shaker South Family Dwelling
and Washshed (c. 1800), Harvard,
Mass. (Robert T. Newman, HABS)

Shaker water tower building
(c. 1820) and interior of the Centre
Family Dwelling House (c. 1820),
Pleasant Hill, Ky. (Lester Jones;
Jack E. Boucher, HABS)

Flower garden (1835), Zoar, Ohio,
designed by the German Separatists. The geometric configuration
represents the New Jerusalem; in
the center is an evergreen tree
representing the Tree of Life.
(Zoar Historical Society)

Communal church building (1871),
West Amana, Iowa, built by the
Amana Society with sandstone
quarried locally. (Cathy Oehl,
Amana Heritage Society)

Women Planting Corn, by Olåf Krans, documenting the shared labor and stringent organization at Bishop Hill, Ill.

Brick residence (c.1860) of a polygamist Mormon family. (Utah State Historical Society)

Logan Temple (1877–84, Truman O. Angell, Sr., and Truman O. Angell, Jr.), with the twin end towers characteristic of Mormon temples. (Utah State Historical Society)

COURTHOUSES
Paul Goeldner

County government, which existed in the English colonies before the Revolution, was well suited to the organization and administration of newly settled lands. An orderly pattern of counties marked the 19th-century passage of the frontier from the Appalachians to the Pacific. Site selection for a courthouse generated the plans for hundreds of county seat towns.

Administrative, judicial and local legislative functions are usually combined in the county courthouse. The architecturally important interior spaces most often are courtrooms, stairs and other areas of public assembly and circulation. Vaults in the offices have the important role of protecting court, land and tax records.

Prominently located and symbolic of economic aspirations, local pride and civic ideals, the courthouse has stimulated its architects to create designs with pacesetting style and technology in their communities. A sequence of styles closely related to stages of economic development appears in different areas without clear regard for dates. After American independence a dominant form for courthouses became the "coffee mill," a two-story, hipped-roof block with a cupola. With modifications and elaborations it remained a perennial model. Jeffersonian political and architectural ideals nourished the Roman and Greek Revivals in American public buildings. Basic details and proportions were within the competency of talented amateur designers and builders nearly everywhere. Adding a dome or cupola to the classic temple form made it a mini-capitol in appearance as well as function. Attaching a classical portico to one or more sides of the "coffee mill" created another form of county capitol.

Unlike Victorian England and Canada, where major public buildings were built in the Gothic style, American

King William County Courthouse (c. 1725), King William, Va. Its arcaded front relieves its stolid appearance. (William Clift, Seagram County Court House Archives, © Library of Congress)

Wise County Courthouse (c. 1895–97, James Riely Gordon), Decatur, Tex., an adaptation of the Richardsonian Romanesque style. (Jim Dow, Seagram County Court House Archives, © Library of Congress)

officials avoided churchly forms for state structures. As courthouse towers became more numerous than domes, their remarkable silhouettes were achieved through ingenious combinations of Italianate, Second Empire, Norman and original motifs but without pointed arches.

H. H. Richardson probably influenced American courthouse design more than any other architect. Posthumous completion of his Allegheny County Courthouse in Pittsburgh in 1888 encouraged other architects to adopt his strong style, to personalize it and to extend it wherever courthouses were being built through the end of the 19th century.

By the turn of the century formal academic training for architects dominated courthouse design with various European Renaissance borrowings. With a few significant exceptions, Beaux-Arts academicism reigned into the depression years. Until the 1920s and 1930s, regionalism had not been a strong influence in courthouse architecture. In areas with significant colonial history, New Deal construction programs encouraged Spanish and Georgian

Montgomery County Courthouse (1847–50, Howard Daniels), Dayton, Ohio, a Greek Revival temple with Ionic columns. (Allen Hess, Seagram County Court House Archives, © Library of Congress)

Beaver County Courthouse (1882), Beaver, Utah, a red brick structure. (Charles D. Harker, HABS)

Cast-iron dome, Old St. Louis Courthouse (1839–62, Singleton and Rumbold), St. Louis. (Frank R. Leslie, HABS)

Macoupin County Courthouse (1867–70, Elijah E. Myers), Carlinville, Ill., a classical design. (William Clift, Seagram County Court House Archives, © Library of Congress)

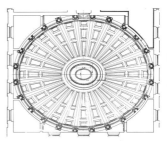

Jury seats, Grady County Courthouse (1908–09, Alexander Blair), Cairo, Ga. (Jim Dow, Seagram County Court House Archives, © Library of Congress)

Woodbury County Courthouse (1916–18, Purcell and Elmslie; William Steele), Sioux City, Iowa, one of the largest Prairie Style buildings ever constructed. (Jack E. Boucher, HABS)

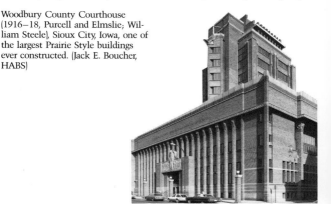

Bartholomew County Courthouse (1871–74, Isaac Hodgson), Columbus, Ind., a dramatic Second Empire–style building. (Bob Thall, Seagram County Court House Archives, © Library of Congress)

Taos County Courthouse (1970, The Architects—Taos), Taos, N.M., recalling the nearby Indian pueblo. (The Architects—Taos)

revival designs for new courthouses and modern blends of classicism, Art Deco and utilitarian frugality elsewhere. Since World War II many new courthouses have been built as commercial office buildings while others have sought traditional symbolism through contemporary forms.

Although some government theorists have proposed that county government is obsolete, courthouses are threatened not by a loss of function but by the functional demands of population increases. Some of the best preservation solutions create county campuses with sympathetic new buildings meeting new requirements. At the center of its community, physically and symbolically, the courthouse dome or tower cannot be removed from the county seat skyline without leaving a hole no water tower can fill. ★

DINERS
Richard J. S. Gutman

No architect ever designed a diner. For more than 100 years, these mobile and modular roadside eateries have been designed and built in factories by tradesmen and craftsmen. Although the first diner was a modified horse-drawn freight wagon, opened in Providence, R.I., in 1872 to serve night lunches only, its immediate success spawned the birth of an industry.

The function of the diner has always been clear-cut: to provide an efficient, economical space in which to prepare, serve and eat food. But the form of the diner has continually changed, evolving to reflect popular culture as interpreted by diner builders.

The 19th-century wagons were ornately decorated examples of the Gilded Era. Their popularity led some operators to seek permanent sites. Simultaneously, a need for more space led manufacturers to produce the first modern diners around 1910. With a counter running the length of the car, the long, narrow form took hold.

Through the 1920s, diners mirrored the modern age, with their use of ceramic tile floors and walls and Monel Metal, a precursor of stainless steel. By 1925 the machine age was visible in many diners' new monitor-style roofs, a direct allusion to streetcar and railroad design.

The golden age of the diner came on the heels of the depression. To reflect forward thinking, diner builders encased the tried-and-true form in the sleekest possible shell, made of stainless steel, porcelain enamel and glass block, achieving a near immobilization of mobility. The interior complemented this streamlined style with heavy use of more stainless steel, Formica, chrome and brightly colored ceramic tile.

Continuous growth in size characterized the evolution of the diner. From a single row of stools, the diner grew in width to include a second row of stools along the window wall. More room allowed table or booth service in the same area. Modular construction in diner building of the 1940s permitted separate dining spaces, and the buildings were then constructed of several parts, shipped separately and joined together on site.

The 1950s saw diners losing all of their vehicular imagery. Facades were dominated by picture windows.

Owl night lunch wagon (c. 1900), Detroit, typical of the early horsedrawn lunch wagons. (Richard J. S. Gutman Collection)

Modern Diner (1940), Pawtucket, R.I., in railroad-car style. (Richard J. S. Gutman Collection)

Tops Diner (c. 1940), Johnstown, Pa., a Streamline Moderne example. (John D. Hesselbein; Richard J. S. Gutman Collection)

Inside, all cooking was relegated to an out-of-sight kitchen. By 1960 historical revival styles had arrived permanently, with exteriors of stone and brick in colonial and Mediterranean styles and interiors to match. With this changeover to the suburban look, roadside diners became family restaurants.

The older diners were readily adapted to alternative uses, affording inexpensive shelter for the small entrepreneur. Examples of some conversions have been barber shops, real estate offices and lawn mower repair shops.

In 1978 the Modern Diner (1940) in Pawtucket, R.I., was named to the National Register of Historic Places. Since then, a greater awareness of this unique American phenomenon has arisen. Most recently, in 1984 the Henry Ford Museum and Greenfield Village in Dearborn, Mich., began to restore the only remaining horse-drawn wagon known to exist. In addition, the museum purchased a 1946 streamlined diner, which will be restored and put back into use as an operating restaurant. ★

Interior of a diner (late 1930s), with highly reflective materials typical of diners of this period. (Richard J. S. Gutman Collection)

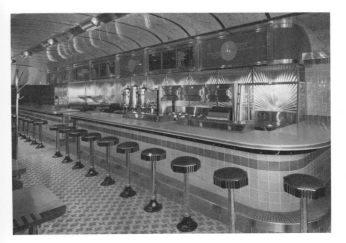

DRIVE-INS
David Gebhard

The array of building types oriented to the automobile—
fast-food places, gasoline stations and drive-in banks, dry
cleaners and theaters as well as retail stores, motels,
churches, tourist cabins and auto campgrounds—has been
integral to the American scene since about 1915. Drive-in
architecture, although neglected in the history of 20th-
century architecture, represents some of this century's
most inventive designs.

Drive-ins were preceded by building types directed
toward the needs of horses, wagons and carriages—livery
stables and blacksmith shops—many of which tended the
needs of the automobile (for gasoline and repairs) in the
early 20th century. Late 19th-century street railway
systems and suburban railroads also dictated the form of
retail commercial development.

Drive-in architecture came into being in four distinct
locales: alongside the highways, parallel to the principal
urban commercial strips, as planned commercial nodules
(which replaced strip development and encompass everything from modest-sized shopping corners to large-scale
regional open or enclosed malls) and off the highway
(resorts and campgrounds). The rise of limited-access
expressways and freeways in the late 1930s further forced
a nodular approach. Moreover, the rapid speed of the car
meant that the drive-in facility had to be visually grasped
by the occupants quickly and indelibly. This was
accomplished by signage that could not be avoided or by
the form of the building itself, which often became its
own sign. By 1941 most of the familiar types of drive-in
architecture had been established. After World War II a
tremendous surge of drive-ins occurred, and by the early
1950s regional shopping centers began to emerge.

The architectural images employed in drive-ins have
mirrored styles in fashion at the moment—regionalism in
the 1920s (colonial for the East, the Pueblo for the
Southwest and the Spanish colonial for Southern California); the Streamline Moderne in the 1930s; and the
universality of the Modern or International Style of the
post-1940s. Now in the 1980s, the regional is once again
being cultivated. The one architectural image that is
almost exclusive to drive-ins is the programmatic (narrative) building [see Ducks and Decorated Sheds].

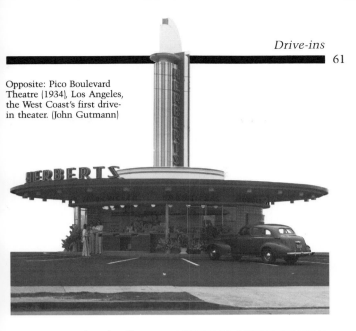

Opposite: Pico Boulevard
Theatre (1934), Los Angeles,
the West Coast's first drive-
in theater. (John Gutmann)

Herbert's Drive-in (1938), Hollywood, Calif., a circular fast-food
restaurant in the Art Deco style.
(Natural History Museum of Los
Angeles County)

McDonnell's Drive-in, Hollywood,
Calif., an early drive-in restaurant.
(John Gutmann)

The McDonald brothers' hamburger stand (1955), Downey, Calif., the oldest
surviving example of the golden arches. (McDonald's Corporation)

Drive-in architecture is, by its nature, ephemeral.
Continually shifting land uses and values and changing
street and highway patterns have meant that only a few of
its major monuments are still in existence. The historically significant supermarkets and shopping centers of
the 1930s and drive-in theaters with the backs of their
high screens often treated with murals and architectural
elements are now increasingly difficult to find.

But a few great examples still remain. The pioneer
regional shopping center—Country Club Plaza (1922–24,
Edward Buehler Delk and Edward W. Tanner) in Kansas
City—is alive and active, as are others. As a building type,
drive-in architecture is still very much with us and has
lost none of its vigor. ★

Jerry's Famous Hot Dogs (1940s), College Park, Md. (Peter Smith, NTHP Collection)

Country Club Plaza (1922–24, Edward Buehler Delk and Edward W. Tanner), Kansas City, Mo., a landmark American shopping center. (J. C. Nichols Company)

Ralph's Supermarket (1940, Stiles O. Clements), Inglewood, Calif., a building transformed into a sign. (David Gebhard)

Drive-in architecture near Bardstown, Ky., 1940—a grocery store, gas station and tourist cabins. (Marion Post Wolcott, FSA)

Opposite: Highway fruit stand, Baton Rouge, La., 1947. (Todd Webb, Standard Oil of New Jersey Collection)

Colonial Cottage Court (1930s), near Louisville, Ky., an early motel. (Marion Post Wolcott, FSA)

Capital Garage (1926, Arthur B. Heaton), Washington, D.C. The largest parking garage in the nation when built, it had 10 stories, 20 parking levels and spaces for 1,300 cars. (John J. G. Blumenson, NTHP)

DUCKS AND DECORATED SHEDS
Steven Izenour

A duck is a duck; it can also be a hot dog, a milk bottle or an elephant. A duck is a building whose function, structure and material are secondary to its representational quality or sculptural form. The building usually looks like what it is selling. Ducks are as old as the Trojan Horse, but only recently have they been rediscovered by architects, artists and architectural historians.

Ducks are sculptural and three-dimensional—the building is the sign. Decorated sheds, on the other hand, are two-dimensional approximations of ducks. The decorated shed exaggerates or distorts one element, usually the front facade, while the rest of the building remains conventional in appearance. The construction and structure of a decorated shed are expedient; in a duck the whole building and structure are distorted to communicate its contents. Classic vernacular examples of the decorated shed are the false front on a western store or the golden arches on a McDonald's of the 1960s.

The term "duck" was coined (together with "decorated shed") in a seminal essay, "A Significance for A&P Parking Lots on Learning from Las Vegas" (1968) by Denise Scott Brown and Robert Venturi and was inspired by the Big Duck (1931), a roadside stand selling ducks in Riverhead, Long Island, N.Y. The Big Duck, like so many examples of this genre, dates from between the world wars, when automobile ownership and highways were expanding at a rapid rate. The early commercial highway strips were more highly competitive visually and economically than recent high-speed highway interchanges, with their homogeneous services and bland regional shopping centers. These first-generation strips were two-lane roads with shorter distances and slower speeds, built before design and sign control. The whimsical ducks could be seen and appreciated while they competed for motorists' attention and dollars.

Along the strip the sign is more important than the building. The sign on the front of a decorated shed is an electrical extravaganza, the building a modest necessity. When the building is the sign—the Big Duck or the Tail o' the Pup—it is both a three-dimensional sculptural symbol and an architectural shelter. The contradiction between outside image—the hot dog—and inside function—the kitchen—is comic; but the building is a powerful sign for attracting attention along the roadside.

The other major location for ducks, in addition to the strip, has always been the resort. From Atlantic City to the Wisconsin Dells, a constant pressure exists to create the next season's attraction. Fantastic make-believe architecture such as Lucy the Elephant (1881), Margate, N.J., is the norm where people step out of their daily lives for a day or a week.

While ducks and decorated sheds are not necessarily great architecture, in the proper context they create humorous relief from the "white bread" good taste of so many of our large-scale urban and suburban developments. They also bring a smile to us all with their idiosyncratic images that evoke nostalgia for a past we enjoy remembering as simpler and crazier. ★

The Big Duck (1931, William Collins), Riverhead, N.Y., the original duck—a retail store selling ducks. (J. J. C. Andrews)

The Pig (1940s), San Antonio, a white stucco structure built as a barbecue stand that later served as a storeroom and a residence. (Carleton Knight III; J. J. C. Andrews)

Lucy the Elephant (1881, William Free), Margate, N.J., a six-story structure built to advertise resort home sites. (Jack E. Boucher)

Tail o' the Pup (1938, Milton J. Black), Los Angeles, a hot dog stand that is the quintessence of Southern California pop architecture. (Carleton Knight III)

Sankey-Hood Milk Bottle (1934), built to sell homemade ice cream, en route from Taunton, Mass., to its new home on the Boston waterfront in 1977.

Holiday Inn (1950s), Las Vegas, Nev., an example of a decorated shed, a building that is its own sign. (Steven Izenour)

Big Do-nut Drive-in (c. 1953), now Randy's Donuts, Los Angeles. (Peter Smith, NTHP Collection)

Hat 'n' Boots (1947), Seattle, built to house a discount store, now adapted as a gas station. The boots are the restrooms. (Carleton Knight III)

"Last Gas Before Freeway" gas station, Houston, in the shape of a gas can. (Daniel Vieyra Collection)

ESTATES
William C. Shopsin

During the 17th-century colonial period, royal land grants established huge manorial estates to entice wealthy gentry to settle, govern and exploit the North American territories. Following the European model, the Dutch patroons in the North and the English planters in the South developed extensive agricultural estates.

Indentured labor and slaves were imported to work the land in the colonies. Plantations were self-contained small communities requiring numerous structures to house the master, the manager, overseers, farm laborers, domestic servants and their families. Monticello (1770–89), Thomas Jefferson's property near Charlottesville, Va., and Philipseburg (1682) and the Van Cortlandt manor houses in Tarrytown, N.Y., are surviving examples of the complex architectural and social organization of the early plantation economy. Stylistically, they reflected the owners' tastes (many brought architectural elements from Europe, such as hardware, chandeliers and decorative objects and furnishings) and the climates of their locale, ranging from the stolid fieldstone northern manor houses of the Dutch patroons to the elegant brick Georgian, Federal and Greek Revival plantation houses of the antebellum South with their familiar white-columned porticoes, such as the Shadows-on-the-Teche, New Iberia, La.

The 19th-century Industrial Revolution and the rising fortunes of urban merchants and manufacturers created a desire for a new type of estate, the country house. The new railroads and steamships made the shorefront resorts accessible. Vast sums were spent to build, furnish and landscape these elegant showplaces. In these elaborate and picturesque settings the merchant princes raised prize-winning farm animals, thoroughbred horses or exotic

Main lodge (1896–97), Camp Sagamore, Sagamore Lake, N.Y., a "rustic" Swiss chalet whose proportions have been expanded to three and a half stories. (Preservation League of New York State)

Lyndhurst (1838, 1864–65, A. J. Davis), Tarrytown, N.Y., an elaborate, castlelike Gothic Revival house. (Jack E. Boucher, HABS)

Opposite: Oak Alley (c. 1830), Vacherie, La., a Greek Revival plantation house. (Balthazar Korab)

plants, as at Lyndhurst (1838, 1864–65), Alexander Jackson Davis's romantic Gothic Revival castle in Tarrytown, N.Y.

Seasonal migrations of the fashionable at the turn of the century might include a farm in Rhinebeck, N.Y., overlooking the Hudson River; a "rustic" camp with a log chalet in the Adirondacks of New York State; or a summer oceanfront villa on a cliff in Newport, R.I., or along the New Jersey coast at Deal or Elberon. Architects such as Richard Morris Hunt and McKim, Mead and White were pleased to oblige. The bulky forms of indoor squash courts, skylighted swimming pools, bowling alleys and covered riding rinks were nestled into the estates, skillfully masked on the exterior by Shingle Style fantasies or eclectic borrowings from the architectural Grand Tour. A pompous Beaux-Arts formalism dominated the axial placement of structures and garden vistas.

In the early 1900s Delano and Aldrich's restrained Georgian Revival and Federal-style country houses set the fashion on Long Island's Gold Coast. The roaring twenties popularized polo and Palm Beach, epitomized by Addison Mizner's medley of haciendas and other Mediterranean villas such as Marjorie Merriweather Post's Mar-a-Lago (1923–27); the resort survived the great stock market crash of 1929 and is still very fashionable.

Post–World War II mobility and the energy crisis have been less kind, especially to houses that have been abandoned and shorn of their acreage, left like beached whales to decay. Fortunately, some of the great estates have been adapted to condominium use by dividing the main house and stable complexes into apartments and discreetly introducing new clustered units within the landscaped grounds. Because the house and the grounds of a historic estate are an inseparable ensemble, the best preservation plans seek to save both while finding a sympathetic new use. ★

The Breakers (1893–95, Richard Morris Hunt), Newport, R.I., a Renaissance-style mansion. The dining room shows the ornate decoration. (Preservation Society of Newport County)

Vizcaya (1916, Hoffman and Chalfin), Miami, with a stone "ship" in the harbor. (Miami-Metro News Bureau)

La Casa Grande (Hearst Castle) (1919, Julia Morgan), San Simeon, Calif., a Moorish-style castle built by William Randolph Hearst. (California Department of Natural Resources)

La Pietra (1919–22, David Adler), Honolulu, modeled on the villa La Pietra in Florence, Italy. The grounds have been subdivided for condominiums, and the mansion now houses the Hawaii School for Girls. (Stan Rivera)

Mar-a-Lago (1923–27, Marion Sims Wyeth), Palm Beach, Fla., representing the Spanish colonial revival at its grandest. (Jack E. Boucher, HABS)

FARMS
William H. Tishler

Since the earliest days of settlement, agriculture has played a major role in shaping the form of America's landscape. The common denominator of this activity was the farm—a tract of land with fields, animals and equipment, dominated by a nucleus of structures representing the farmstead. These agrarian buildings portray what are perhaps the most diverse elements of our nation's built environment.

Essentially a complex for growing, processing and storing crops and livestock, the farm became a unique physical expression of its owner or builder. The house and barn served as key structures, and their relationship to other buildings and service areas grew from decisions based on the farmer's ingenuity and the influence of function, tradition, available building materials, cost considerations and environmental factors such as topography and drainage, access, microclimate and sources of water. Accessory buildings were built to accommodate additional shelter and storage needs. These varied in both number and form, depending on the nature of the farming operation, the region of the country and the owner's cultural background. They might have included domestic structures such as the summer kitchen, bake oven, smoke house, privy, ice house, spring house and root cellar; stock shelters such as the stable, piggery, chicken coop and sheep barn; crop storage facilities, including the granary, hay barn, corn crib, silo, tobacco barn and hop house; and structures used primarily for work activities, among them

Farm complex, Stephenson County, Ill., showing alternating contour strips of corn and alfalfa planted to reduce soil erosion. (Tim McCabe, Soil Conservation Service, USDA)

a woodshed, toolshed, machine shed and blacksmith shop, to round out the complement of buildings.

Fostered by isolation and a subsistence economy, early colonists and immigrant groups initially adhered to familiar Old World methods of farming and building. But new crops and trends in agriculture, an abundance of cheap land parcelled from the land survey grid, the availability of standardized construction materials and growing acceptance of new building concepts revolutionized the farmstead. As a result, the form and size of farms changed as settlement pushed westward and husbandmen adapted to the new conditions of their young and dynamic country. Another influence on the evolving form of agrarian complexes was the growing number of farm journals and handbooks. Read by many progressive farmers, they espoused improved farming techniques and frequently included advice on the planning and construction of rural buildings and hints for arranging and beautifying the farmstead. Later, land grant universities and the U.S. Department of Agriculture provided literature and advice that spearheaded farm planning and rural improvement.

By the end of World War I, new and dramatic forces began to reshape American agriculture. This evolution was reflected in the form and spatial organization of the farm. With the advent of new technology that included barbed wire, the metal windmill, the gasoline-powered

Residence of J. M. Hayner, Lebanon, Ohio, showing farm buildings in close proximity to the main house. (NTHP Collection)

The Cornell Farm, by Edward Hicks, depicting a farm in Bucks County, Pa. (National Gallery of Art)

Citrus estate, near Westlaw, Tex., 1948. (Russell Lee, Standard Oil of New Jersey Collection)

tractor and rural electrification, farms began to increase in size, but the number and type of traditional structures in the rural complex began to decrease as their functions became obsolete.

The observer of today's rural countryside finds change running rampant. Everywhere, the familiar features of the farm landscape are disappearing as big agribusinesses and absentee landlords take over the control of more rural land. The implications of this change include a continuing decrease in the number of farms, roadside strips of highway architecture screening off the countryside behind them, concentration of agricultural production on our better land with enlarged field patterns of monoculture crops and a new silhouette for the industrialized and highly mechanized farmstead. As the visible reminders of our agrarian heritage disappear, we lose an important part of ourselves and our roots to the land. ★

"View of Model Farm Buildings for a Maine Farmer," the cover illustration for an 1857 article endorsing connected farm buildings.

Farm with a windmill, often a standard farm structure. (William H. Tishler)

A 400-acre, strip-cropped dairy farm, Stanton, Mich. (Erwin W. Cole, Soil Conservation Service, USDA)

FENCES
John Fraser Hart

Farmers knew that good fences make good neighbors long before Robert Frost immortalized this particular bit of folk wisdom in "Mending Wall." The purpose of a fence is to protect crops, to restrain animals, to define territorial ownership or all of these. Fences keep animals out of cultivated fields, where they do not belong, and within the pastures and grazing areas where they do belong.

Legal doctrines reflect these functions. Fence laws in farming areas, where crops are important, require owners to enclose their animals, but ranching areas have open range laws that permit stock to roam at will and require farmers to protect their crops.

The style of a fence reflects vernacular traditions, the availability of building materials and the needs of the local economy. In the wooded East pioneers made fences from the trees they had to clear from the land before they could cultivate it. They erected zig-zag fences by laying split rails one on top of another at right angles. Later farmers constructed straight post-and-rail fences by inserting horizontal rails in holes bored in rows of vertical posts. Gentleman farmers protected the hides of their valuable animals by making fences of wooden boards, which they painted white.

Settlers on the treeless prairie grasslands experimented with hedgerows of Osage orange before barbed wire was invented in the early 1870s. Ecologically fragile range areas in the subhumid West could not have been settled without barbed wire, which ranchers use to control grazing by cattle and horses.

Barbed wire will not stop hogs, and farmers in the agricultural heartland had to have hog-proof fences,

An unusual stone wall leading to Biltmore, Asheville, N.C. (Balthazar Korab)

Split-rail fence, Salem, N.C., the standard pioneer fence wherever wood was available. Riders were set at angles to keep the top rail from falling off. (Balthazar Korab)

because every field had to serve as a grazing area at some time in the crop rotation. The standard fence in the Midwest was made of woven wire (often called hog wire) set on steel posts and topped by a strand or two of barbed wire. Many farmers in the Midwest removed their fences when they switched to cash grain farming or to confined feeding of hogs and cattle. They can run strands of electrified wire on metal posts when they need a cheap temporary fence.

The cotton, tobacco and peanut fields of the South did not need fences, and farmers who have introduced beef cattle in the region have had to bear the cost of fencing their land.

Stone walls are rare except in the glaciated areas of New England or in places where limestone and sandstone form natural flagstones, because the construction of a stone wall requires cheap labor and an abundance of the right kind of stone. Even rarer are stump fences on sandy outwash plains at the edge of the Great North Woods, where early settlers uprooted white pine stumps and turned them on their sides. Most stump fences have disappeared because, like other wooden fences, they catch fire and burn so easily.

Fences in nonagricultural areas display a bewildering variety. Most of them are designed for exclusion and security, for privacy or for ornamentation. Heavy-gauge wire mesh on stout metal posts is the most common type of security fence, although high stone walls can perform the same function. High hedges, stone walls or tall board fences can provide privacy. Ornamental fences may be made of stone, hedge, boards, rails, pickets, cast iron or a whole host of other materials—the only constraint on their materials and design seems to be the imagination of their builders and owners. ★

Picket fence, Coburn Tyler House (c. 1850), Camden, Maine, an especially intricate variation on a common residential type. (Cervin Robinson, HABS)

Cast-iron fence in the cornstalk pattern (1859, Wood and Perot), New Orleans. Many urban fences are as decorative as they are functional. (Dan Leyrer, HABS)

FIREHOUSES
Rebecca Zurier

The story of the American firehouse is part of that peculiar social institution, the American fire company. The buildings' size, shape and character reflect the organization's development from a voluntary association— a cross between a lodge and a baseball team—into a branch of municipal government. Eighteenth-century firehouses were simply places to store a town's supply of fire engines, buckets, hooks and ladders. Built in an easily accessible location, the firehouse could be a plain wooden shed or incorporated into a larger public structure—usually brick but sometimes stone—that served several functions. As responsibility for fire protection shifted from the community at large to private, fraternal companies, firehouses took on the character of clubhouses, with lavish second-story meeting rooms over the garage. Before long, the buildings themselves came to be seen as flamboyant architectural emblems—as distinctive a part of the company's regalia as its uniform. Hose-drying towers, introduced in the 1840s, became an identifying feature, along with oversized garage doors, red paint and an abundance of lettering and other insignia.

Changes in the administration and procedures of the fire service around the time of the Civil War altered the size and shape of firehouses. Exasperated with the rowdy antics of volunteer firemen, city governments set up paid, paramilitary fire departments and built engine houses that replaced the clubrooms with dormitories for full-time crews. The horse-drawn steam fire engines developed in the 1860s required an expanded ground-floor apparatus room that could serve as a combined garage, machine shop and stable. Living quarters and offices were moved upstairs to segregate the men from the horses.

This hybrid of functions combining public and private, institutional and domestic has determined the fire station's program ever since. For prototypes, city architects looked no longer to the private clubhouse but to commercial and industrial architecture, resulting in buildings with a more uniform, utilitarian appearance. In downtown areas where land was at a premium, small stations built to hold one or two pieces of equipment copied the facades of storefront or urban carriage houses. New communities offered sites large enough for barnlike structures housing several engine, hose and ladder companies under one roof. Firehouses of the 1880s were filled with automatic gadgets designed to speed response to an alarm—including the sliding pole, invented by a Chicago fireman in 1878.

The turn-of-the-century firehouse achieved a new civic grandeur as architects turned to European sources to convey a sense of municipal presence. Some evoked regional styles: Spanish in Southern California, neo-colonial in the suburbs of Boston and stepped-gable Dutch in New York State. Stations in the new streetcar suburbs took their cues from the large homes nearby. The one-story bungalow firehouses designed after 1912 were a response to pressure from residents of middle-class neighborhoods for modest buildings that blended in. They owed their size and shape to the compact automobile-powered equipment that did away with the need for

Hibernia Fire Engine Company, No. 1, Philadelphia, with its volunteer firemen—part lodge, part athletic team, part militia—assembled in front about 1857. (P. S. Duval and Sons, Historical Society of Pennsylvania)

horses and allowed living quarters to be moved to the ground floor. When a change in the work schedule required firemen to take their meals at the station, kitchens were added and the atmosphere became even more homelike.

After World War II, fire departments began to group several companies in one sprawling building, often sited at the edge of town. A one-story plan that eliminated the hazardous sliding pole allowed quicker access to the engine room from all parts of the building and accommodated larger equipment. Today, firehouses recall little traditional imagery: Hose-drying machines have replaced the towers, wide roll-up garage doors resemble those on gas stations, and even the use of flags and lettering has gone out of favor. But the buildings' role as unofficial social center lives on, as does the firefighter's place in popular mythology. ★

Head House (c. 1804) at New Market, Philadelphia, built to house an engine and a hose company. (A. Pierce Bounds)

Engine Company No. 33 (1888, Arthur H. Vinal), Boston. The round arches and rough textures epitomize the Richardsonian Romanesque style. (A. Pierce Bounds)

Fire Station No. 14 (1913, Morgan and Dillon), Atlanta, designed to look like a bungalow. (Courtesy Chief Steve B. Campbell)

Hook and Ladder Company No. 4 (1910, Marcus T. Reynolds), Albany, N.Y., with stepped gables indicating a Dutch stylistic influence. (Theresa Beyer, Library of Congress)

Fair Play Fire Engine and Hose Company No. 1 (c. 1875, 1888), Madison, Ind., home of Indiana's oldest volunteer fire company. The "Little Jimmy" weathervane is the company's trademark. (Richard Berliner, HABS)

Engine Company No. 1 (1940), Los Angeles. With its fins, band windows, horizontal grooves and projections, this station is a classic example of Streamline Moderne. (Architectural Archives, Santa Barbara)

Fire Station No. 4 (1965–67, Venturi and Rauch), Columbus, Ind., a spare modern fire station with a prominent symbolic tower. (David Hirsch)

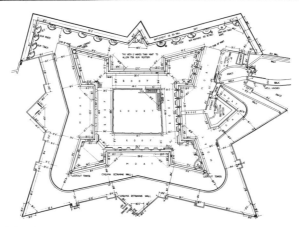

FORTS
Willard B. Robinson

Essential to the security of life and protection of land claims, countless forts were erected in America by both the military and civilians. The first colonists relied on enclosures of logs and earth, exemplified by the triangular and turreted enclosure of pickets at Jamestown. As colonization by England, Spain and France progressed, these first forts were replaced by durable masonry works, designed by military engineers employing European Renaissance concepts of design. Commonly square, these incorporated bastions on each corner, providing flanks from which the fort's curtain and collateral bastions could be defended; an outstanding example is Fort Ticonderoga (begun 1755), Ticonderoga, N.Y., a French work.

In the Southwest, Spanish military detachments erected a number of presidios. Commonly built of adobe, little remains of most of these. Also significant are numerous forts built by fur traders and pioneers. These were simple in form and expedient in construction, employing materials at hand.

After the Revolutionary War, the fortification of sea frontiers was considered vital to American national security. Under the direction of several French engineers, a series of forts, including Fort Sewall (1794), Marblehead, Mass., was constructed with earth, timber and masonry. Consisting of batteries, barracks and hot-shot ovens for heating cannon balls, these were small and would have been ineffective against attack.

Following the War of 1812, Congress commissioned the French engineer Simon Bernard to fortify American coasts with a system of forts. Employing French theory on the art of fortification, General Bernard designed a series of masonry forts containing artillery, garrisons and magazines. Strategically located and designed to protect key commercial cities from attack by sea and usually by land, they commonly incorporated features such as ditches (moats), bastions and casemates, the latter a vaulted bombproof enclosure.

Joseph G. Totten, a graduate of the U.S. Military Academy, was next placed in charge of national fortifications. Under his direction forts were completed and several new ones, noteworthy for masonry work, were begun using plans based on evolving French theory on military architecture. Among these, Fort Point (1853) was

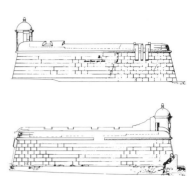

Opposite: Castillo San Marcos (Fort Marion) (1565), St. Augustine, Fla., built of local coquina rock and exhibiting classic bastion, moat and drawbridge features. (J. Erwin Page, HABS)

El Cañuelo (c. 1520), Cabras Island, San Juan, Puerto Rico, an early Spanish fort of field-stone covered with plaster. (Frederik C. Gjessing, HABS)

a multitiered work designed to mount numerous smooth-bore cannons to defend San Francisco Bay.

However, at mid-19th century, with the invention of high-powered rifled cannons with considerable range and destructive capabilities, all these immediately became obsolete, a fact that was well demonstrated during the Civil War at Fort Pulaski (1829), Cockspur Island, Ga., and Fort Sumter (1829), Charleston, S.C.

At the same time, numerous forts intended to enforce frontier protection against Indian uprisings were built. Although some, such as Fort Reno (1865), Wyo., were fortified enclosures, many were simply open complexes of buildings organized around a parade ground, reflecting military discipline. Among the latter group are Fort Laramie (1849), Wyo., and Fort Davis (1859), Tex.

At the turn of the 20th century, numerous new works were built by the federal government for defense of our seacoasts. Massive concrete parapets protected newly developed long-range cannons and rapid-firing guns, while rooms for ammunition and troops were contained within thick reinforced concrete walls and roofs. Many of America's forts have been restored and are now maintained and interpreted by federal and state agencies. ★

Fort McHenry (1794–1803), Baltimore. During the War of 1812 it withstood bombardment by a British fleet, inspiring Francis Scott Key to write "The Star-Spangled Banner." (M. E. Warren)

Plan of Fort Union (c. 1850), N.M., showing the officers' quarters, company quarters and post corral. (National Archives)

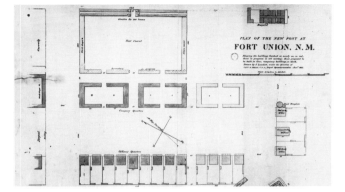

Cannon porthole, Fort Pulaski (1829), Cockspur Island, Ga., commandeered briefly by the Confederate troops during the Civil War. (National Park Service)

Fort Adams (1824–45), Providence, one of the most complex ensembles of military architectural forms in this country when built. (Rhode Island Department of Natural Resources)

Fort Laramie (1849), Wyo., sited between two branches of the Laramie River. (National Archives)

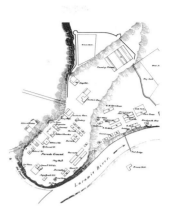

Officers' Quarters (1905–06), Fort Sam Houston, San Antonio, a standardized design with a porch adapted to the warm climate. (David J. Kaminsky, HABS)

GAS STATIONS
Daniel I. Vieyra

Out of the need to service the automobile developed a building type that would become a ubiquitous cultural landmark—the gasoline station. The modern gas station did not burst full-blown on the American scene but evolved gradually from a crude row of elevated tanks to a slick representation of corporate image.

Early motorists treated their cars like horses, feeding them petroleum obtained from drums at the local livery, hardware or dry goods store. Ironically, tank wagons that delivered gasoline to these retail establishments from local distribution centers known as bulk plants were drawn by horses. Eventually, price-conscious motorists began bypassing traditional gasoline dealers in favor of a trip directly to the bulk station. The resulting station became the corporate package that had to convey the advantages of the oil company's unseen product.

A series of themes emerged in this at once highly sophisticated and disarmingly simple building type, each catching motorists' attention in a distinctive manner.

The earliest image projected by the gas station was a "fantastic" one, emphatically attracting attention in a naive way. Such stations, which emerged in the 1920s and remained in vogue through the early 1940s, were built in the shape of boats, lighthouses, airplanes and space stations. Buildings taking the form of gas pumps, measuring and gas cans, tank cars and three-dimensional representations of company trademarks glorified automobile transportation. Filling stations in the form of icebergs, southern mammies, tipis and pagodas portrayed natural formations, cultural themes and exotic architecture.

Creating an aura of prestige and making an imposing addition to the roadside, "respectable" stations, which emerged in the late 1950s and early 1960s, bestowed prestige on their brand of gas. Receiving their impetus from the City Beautiful movement, these stations were part of the drive to make the structure a civic asset; they thus used architectural features associated with buildings of great civic importance.

Suggesting the values of hearth and home, the "domestic" station blended with neighboring residences while serving as a symbol of familiarity to the traveler in an unfamiliar area. These stations ranged from the rustic, irregular cottage with ties to the English picturesque movement to standardized company models. The more recent generation of "domestic" stations, given an impetus from Lady Bird Johnson's beautification in the 1960s, reflected their suburban surroundings in the form of ranch and split-level structures.

When first introduced, the "functional" filling station was hailed as a building that had the inestimable virtue of looking like what it was. Frank Lloyd Wright, Richard Neutra, Rudolph Schindler, Bertrand Goldberg and William Lescaze were among the prominent architects involved in the design of these modern stations. Another approach to modern design was the Moderne, featuring curves suggesting speed and an aesthetic of futurism, as executed by industrial designers. Norman Bel Geddes, Raymond Loewy and Walter Dorwin Teague all produced Streamline Moderne extravaganzas.

Central Oil and Gasoline Station (1910), Detroit, featuring a separate shed, modern pumps feeding directly to the cars and a drive-through lot. *(National Petroleum News)*

Gas stations, once considered all too common, are now becoming an endangered species. Many of the early small stations without enclosed service bays have become functionally obsolete. With oil companies constantly updating their own images and marketing strategies, even the more recent stations face an uncertain future. A number of old stations have been listed in the National Register of Historic Places. Successful rebirth through adaptive use involves the incorporation of the station's most prominent characteristic—its image—into the new form. The gas station, itself the premier drive-in building, has a history and rich design heritage of its own and is a significant part of the built environment. ★

Hartford Garage Company (c. 1920), Hartford, Conn. Around 1905 a gravity-fed system using hoses replaced the bucket as a means of refueling. (Texaco, Inc.)

A combination dry goods store and
filling station (c. 1920), Onondaga,
N.Y. (Shell Oil Company)

A 1926 advertisement for a prefabricated station, one of a dozen planning
designs for an ornamental gas station offered by Union Metal Manufactur-
ing Company. *(National Petroleum News)*

Opposite: "Drum" station pro-
totype for Mobil Oil (c. 1940,
Frederick Frost), New York City.
(Mobil Oil Corporation)

Shell Station (1930–33, J. H. Glenn, Jr., and Bert L. Bennett), Winston-Salem, N.C., a white concrete "fantastic" station now serving as an engine repair shop. (Joann Sieburg, N.C. Division of Archives and History)

Gravity-fed Shell gas pump (c. 1920), Cannelton, Ind. (Jack E. Boucher, HABS)

Pure Oil Station (1930s), Columbus, Ohio, a two-bay "domestic" station. (Union Oil Company of California)

HOSPITALS
John D. Thompson

The building of hospitals came fairly late to the British colonies that were to become the United States. The first was the Pennsylvania Hospital, begun in 1756 and completed in 1805. In spite of the later start, hospital architecture in America followed the same developmental stages as in Europe. Four distinct phases of hospital design —the derivative, the pavilion, the skyscraper and the healing factory—created an identifiable form of architecture reflecting changes in the science of medicine as well as in the social role of the hospital itself.

The first or derivative phase is so named because the hospitals adopted their forms from those of other public buildings. Although there were some unique features—for example, the inclusion of an amphitheater in the dome— hospitals appeared in many styles from Georgian to the early Stick Style. Charles Bulfinch's Massachusetts General (1818) was first designed as a building for Harvard College, and when Ithiel Town received the commission to build a hospital in New Haven in 1832, he was instructed to design one resembling the Gothic Revival Episcopalian Chapel. Town demurred and informed the board that he would build it in the style of the old statehouse (Greek Revival), which was then located in New Haven.

This eclecticism arose because the style of each building reflected the visions of the hospital's founders rather than a form designed for the care of patients. These were hospitals for the poor and homeless; they were considered as venerable charities and so were given an appropriate appearance. Furthermore, no theory existed to relate the design of the building to the health of the patients.

This lack of a connecting rationale disappeared when the lessons from the Crimean War and, in the United States, the Civil War were absorbed by those concerned with public health and sanitary reform. The next design phase, the pavilion or barracks system, was promoted by

Mower General Hospital (1865, John McArthur, Jr.), Philadelphia, a temporary military hospital whose plan was adopted in Germany during the Franco-Prussian War. (Fry Print Collection, Yale Medical Library)

Florence Nightingale in response to the miasma theory of disease causality, which held that patients should be exposed only to clean air free from the miasma of disease. Architecturally, the theory was translated into a series of detached pavilions connected by a traffic corridor, and great care was exercised to prevent the air from one building from passing into another. The foremost example of this form was the old Johns Hopkins Hospital (1877–85), Baltimore.

The architectural form of these pavilion hospitals was just as clear as the medical rationale behind it. The wards were the most visible feature. The only question was whether these separate wards should be built of one story, two stories or more. Very few of these pavilion-type hospitals remain, although occasionally an isolated pavilion can be found, usually surrounded by later buildings.

The next development was the skyscraper phase, considered by Europeans as a typical American solution; it owed its development primarily to the invention of the elevator. This design permitted the stacking of the formerly dispersed wards one on top of the other and allowed easy access to X-ray and operating rooms, which were becoming as important a feature as the wards. These floors differed from the previous units in that they contained not so much open wards as various mixtures of single two-bed and four-bed rooms. In viewing these first skyscraper hospitals, with the exception of New York Hospital (1933), the functional elements were still quite visible. On top of a platform that contained the assortment of operating rooms and laboratories were stacked the wards or patient floors to a height of 10 to 14 stories. The major design option was the configuration of the patient floors—in an X shape, H shape, Greek cross or double corridor design.

The last phase was brought about by changes in the way patients were treated in the modern hospital. As the average length of stay fell and as the former patient unit began to be divided into various kinds of special case units, such as coronary care, postsurgery care and intensive care, exact replication of a single patient floor

Lincoln Hospital (1860s), Washington, D.C., a Civil War hospital in which tents for infectious cases housed half the patients. (Fry Print Collection, Yale Medical Library)

State Asylum for the Insane (1860), Tuscaloosa, Ala., a linear hospital based on plans by Dr. Thomas S. Kirkbride. The far wings were reserved for violent patients.

Floor plan of Pennsylvania Hospital (1751–1805), Philadelphia, the first voluntary hospital in the United States. It was built in a modified H plan based on the plan of the Edinburgh Royal Infirmary. (Spangler and Davis)

Massachusetts General Hospital (1818–23, Charles Bulfinch), Boston, the original building of the hospital with its signature Ether Dome. The dome room is a lecture hall. (Massachusetts General Hospital)

became more and more difficult. As a consequence, the form of the hospital lost its identifiable patient floors and became indistinguishable from the shape of various other types of buildings. In some instances, a rather large atrium was built at the center of the building, which permitted patients on the inside corridors to have a window in their rooms. Patients in these hospitals are usually quite sick; the amenities are giving way to high technology in a carefully controlled healing factory. ★

Old Johns Hopkins Hospital
(1877–85, John Niernsee and Cabot
and Chandler), Baltimore, a Gothic
Revival complex. (M. E. Warren)

U.S. Naval Medical Center
(1940–42, Frederic W. Southworth
and Paul Cret), Bethesda, Md., an
Art Deco skyscraper. (Hans Wirz,
Smithsonian Institution)

Memorial Unit (1952, 1971–72, Douglas, Orr, Orr, Winder and DeCossy),
Yale–New Haven Hospital, New
Haven, Conn., a modern healing
factory. (Yale–New Haven Hospital)

HOUSES
Charles W. Moore

From the beginning of American settlement, the free-standing single-family house has been at the center of the national dream. The earliest houses combined memories of those in England or Europe with canny adaptation to new climates: A big central chimney conserved heat in cold New England winters; a central hall encouraged breezes through the house during sultry southern summers. In the Southwest, Spain and the Caribbean provided models for houses built around a patio or with verandahs.

As cities along the eastern seaboard grew in population, they were built solid. Houses came to the street, shared side walls and sometimes even collided with their neighbors on the street behind. Boston, New York, Philadelphia, Baltimore, Washington and smaller cities were built densely, mostly of row houses and tenements, through the 18th century and most of the 19th. After 1870 a series of inventions—the horse car, the streetcar, the bicycle and, most notably, the automobile—opened up access to the cheap land lying beyond the towns and allowed for freestanding houses again.

Few American houses are huge or built for the ages. Wood construction—quick, cheap and relatively short-lived—is favored almost everywhere in the United States. Ornament, however, is preferred, as is space around the house and in front of it—the bigger the dimension, the more important the house.

Perhaps the most profound influence on the American house in the early 19th century came from Thomas Jefferson, who helped usher in a Roman revival, which gradually became the Greek Revival and, with porticoes and classical orders, ennobled houses throughout the century. The Greek Revival became an almost universal style. It was challenged, by mid-19th century, by proponents of Gothic design. After Gothic came late Victorian exuberances.

When the architectural revolution came, it was in the realm of the house. By the 1890s Frank Lloyd Wright and other architects were building houses for the midwestern prairie and the Chicago suburbs in which spaces flowed together under wide hovering roofs, perhaps pinned to the site by a central mass of masonry.

Monticello (1770–89, Thomas Jefferson), Charlottesville, Va., a laboratory for Jefferson's ideas. (John J. G. Blumenson, NTHP)

Jethro Coffin House (c. 1686), Nantucket, Mass., typical of early New England houses with its central chimney, shingle covering and lean-to, or saltbox, configuration. (Cortlandt V. D. Hubbard, HABS)

More traditional architectural idioms would reappear, but the house would never be quite the same again. The typical American house came down to one story. It faced the street and opened up to a private, inhabitable yard, usually in the back. The automobile often took over the space on the front lawn; a giant double driveway leading to a wide garage door was often the largest object on the front elevation. This aperture had to be accommodated, so the prevailing shape became a garage-dominant ell. Plans were frequently inverted to put the living rooms toward the back yard.

In the early 1970s, after the oil embargo, energy was no longer cheap, and glass walls became solid again. About the same time, cheap land began to vanish. The typical suburban house, which just after World War II might have been 800 square feet in area, with two bedrooms and a bath, had grown to perhaps twice that size, on a large piece of land, with three bedrooms, two baths and a family room. Stylistically the "modern" vs. "traditional" controversies of decades past appear to have dissolved into a variety of combinations and persuasions in between. "Eclecticism" seems to have swept the day.

Houses are bound to get smaller and, perhaps, to come up again to their lot lines (as do patio houses, zero-lot-line houses and condominiums). Meanwhile, the mobile home has taken over an increasing share of new housing construction. With its illusion of mobility, its simplicity and relative economy, it suggests dimensions of the American dream that we have only begun to discover. ★

Eldridge Johnson House (The Pink House) (1882), Cape May, N.J., a Carpenter Gothic confection. (Perry Benson, HABS)

Houses on Stockton Row (1880s), Cape May, N.J. Cape May is a treasure trove of Gothic Revival architecture. (Jack E. Boucher, HABS)

Bebb (Octagonal) House (1865), Washington, D.C., a house type that flourished in the mid-19th century. (HABS)

Johnston-Hay House (1855–60), Macon, Ga., a grand house in the Italianate style. (Drinnon Studio, HABS)

John C. McConnell House (1883), Cape May, N.J., a vigorously detailed Queen Anne–style house. (Hugh McCauley, HABS)

Bungalow in the Hanchett Residence Park (1910s), San Jose, Calif. Bungalows provided simple and affordable middle-class housing. (Barbara Friedman and John Murphy, HABS)

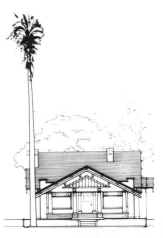

Four-square house (c. 1915), Carlisle, Pa., a post-Victorian response to the desire for simpler middle-class housing. (Dell Upton)

Pope-Leighey House (1940–41, Frank Lloyd Wright), Mount Vernon, Va., a Usonian design for people of "modest means." (Wm. Edmund Barrett)

Kitchen (1940s), Brown-Wagner House (1894), Brownsville, Tex., a remodeled kitchen typical of the period. (Bill Engdahl, Hedrich-Blessing, HABS)

INDIAN SETTLEMENTS
Bob Easton

Europeans exploring North America 500 years ago discovered a well-populated continent containing many forms of native settlement. Their recorded observations form the basis of our knowledge of Indian society at the advent of the historic period. Archeology has yielded evidence of prehistoric settlements larger than those of the historic period. Moreover, eroded mounds in the midwestern and southern United States and stone cliff dwellings in the Southwest indicate the presence of well-developed early cultures.

Indian settlements of the historic period varied with region and tribe and can generally be classified as sedentary, semisedentary and seminomadic. Almost always the winter village was the "central place," or permanent settlement. Typically, in the spring and summer it would be vacated (to varying degrees) as the Indians moved to favorite camping grounds to hunt, fish and gather food and live more comfortably during the hot months.

Permanent settlements were usually located near waterways and fertile soils and in areas sheltered from severe weather. In many regions, they were also sited or palisaded for defensive purposes. Some villages were organized about central plazas with and without ceremonial structures; others were simply collections of houses lined up or randomly grouped. The form of these settlements (and houses as well) was shaped by cultural forces—e.g., a tribe's historical migrations, social customs, religious beliefs and economic practice—as well as by climate and environment. Most tribal groups within the same culture area built and lived differently even though their environment provided the same materials, sustenance and climate.

At the time of European contact, the woodlands region of the Northeast contained two major linguistic groups, the Iroquois and Algonquin. The villages of the sedentary Iroquois consisted of many randomly arranged longhouses that were sometimes up to 300 feet long, housing

Pueblo Bonito (c. 1100), Chaco Canyon, N.M., an artist's rendering of this stone settlement based on its recovered foundations. (T. Sinclair and Son, Smithsonian Institution)

extended families and typically ringed by palisades. Entire villages would relocate every 15 to 20 years because of depleted soil and timber. The semisedentary coastal Algonquin built smaller longhouses at inland winter villages sheltered in the forest and lived in the ubiquitous domed wigwam along the coast in the summertime. Both groups built with bark lashed to a bent sapling frame.

In the Southeast, major Creek and Cherokee setttlements consisted of family house compounds neatly arranged around a central plaza that contained an open, four-sided ceremonial meeting structure, a round conical-roof winter meetinghouse and a ball court that usually contained a vestigial mound. Building materials were saplings, wattle and daub, and thatch.

The introduction of the horse to the Plains and Plateau Indians enabled them to follow migrating buffalo herds, changing many tribes' semisedentary life to an almost nomadic one. Large canvas tipis became year-round houses and were arranged in circles sometimes a mile in circumference for summer ceremonial gatherings. The semisubterranean circular earth lodge settlements of the northern plains Mandan were organized around a central plaza, with the ceremonial "okipa" lodge axially facing the centrally located timber "long man" shrine.

The semisedentary tribes of the Pacific Northwest region built settlements of split cedar or redwood plank

Crow tipi circle, Great Plains, c. 1900, measuring one mile in circumference. (Walter McClintock, Yale University Library)

houses lining sheltered coves. The chief's house was centrally located, and, in many cases, a plank "street" ran along the housefronts, separating them from the canoe-lined beach.

The pueblos of the Southwest, along with tipis, are the best-known type of Indian settlement. They stand as mud and timber symbols of prehistoric times, but they are, in fact, complex series of domestic communal and religious spaces layered with patterns of changing use. Their forms are aesthetically pleasing and seem organic to their environment, and their usual arrangement about a plaza facilitates a sense of place during ceremonial dances. Occupying the same desert environment were the Navajo and Apache, who lived a semisedentary life in family homestead settlements or small tribal groups.

Indian settlements reflect the change and conflict found within Indian society today. Rows of government houses placed in suburban street layouts or dilapidated houses characterize many reservation settlements. Traditionalists are reviving interest in the old house types with recently constructed examples standing on many reservations, and major pueblos are being restored with government assistance. ★

Kickapoo camp, southern Great Plains, c. 1890, showing wigwams covered with reed mats. (Oklahoma Historical Society)

Terraced adobe houses, Zuni Pueblo, Zuni, N.M.

Taos Pueblo, Taos, N.M., c. 1926, with Indians gathered for a San Geronimo Day celebration. (Bob Easton Collection)

Chino (Wintu) village, near Redding, Calif., composed of subterranean earth lodge dwellings. (H. B. Brown, Bancroft Library, University of California)

Montezuma Castle (1250), Arizona, a five-story, 20-room structure built by Sinagua Indians. (National Park Service)

Haida Village, Queen Charlotte Island, B.C., c. 1880. The totem poles are mortuary poles explaining the lineage of the clan that owns the house. (Museums of Canada)

Shepherd's Mill (c. 1739), Shepherdstown, W. Va., an overshot gristmill with a 40-foot iron water wheel. (Belmont Freeman, HAER)

Lower Pacific Mills (c. 1875), Lawrence, Mass. (© Randolph Langenbach)

Whitney Arms Company (c. 1798), Hamden, Conn., Eli Whitney's musket factory, which used division of labor and power-driven machinery. (Van Slyck, HAER)

Gruber Wagon Works (1882, 1906), near Bernville, Pa., a factory built and operated as a family business. (Roland David Schaaf, HAER)

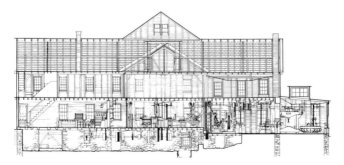

INDUSTRIAL STRUCTURES
Robert M. Vogel

No single building type exists in a greater profusion of scales, styles, shapes, materials and other variables than industrial structures. This nearly limitless variation is due to the equally limitless nature of industry itself, which ranges from the infinitely delicate—plants no larger than houses—to massive, amorphously styled mills (not to mention "public" industrial buildings such as railroad stations and others, which process mainly people).

The greatest contrasts among industrial structures are found in the industries that handle bulk materials, which occur in such disparate forms as liquids, semiliquids, sludges, powders, grains, lumps, sheets, slabs, strips, logs and large, heavy solid masses—all of which must in a hundred different ways be manipulated, lifted, moved about, shipped and stored. Less varied are the buildings that house essentially assembling industries, the factories that produce both hard and soft goods, food products and other manufactured goods. Industrial structures most commonly seen fall into two broad types: buildings (enclosures of space) and nonbuildings.

The most prevalent type of industrial building is the nonspecific factory of one or more stories. The general configuration, materials and architectural features have followed a fairly clearly established path of evolution. Factories of the 19th century were of frame, brick or stone, with small windows because of their bearing-wall construction. Roofs were pitched until the 1870s, often low-pitched or flat thereafter. In the late 19th century, the iron and then steel structural frame appeared and, shortly afterward, the reinforced concrete frame, freeing the exterior walls of their structural function and permitting larger windows.

As water power gave way to steam and then electric drive, the factory site was freed of the restrictions imposed by such hydraulic features as power canals and dams, resulting in wider buildings with fewer stories. This trend was the result, also, of increasingly efficient artificial light sources (gas and electric), which meant that it was less essential for machinery and workers to be located near windows. Today, most factories are a single story, which eliminates the vertical handling of materials and people, and windowless, which reduces capital cost, maintenance and heat loss and gain.

Such generally nondistinctive buildings, which process materials or manufacture products where the raw materials, the production machinery and the finished product are not of great size, include textile mills, most food-processing plants and manufactories for small machinery, clothing and other products. With larger product size—heavy machinery, automobiles, steel and lumber, for example—the size of the building's structural bays increases, the roof structure is heavier as trusses become necessary to span the greater distances, and the floor heights increase to accommodate large machinery and overhead cranes.

A second general class of industrial building, less common, is that whose sole function is to protect from the weather nonmanufacturing or processing machines. The function usually is clear from the setting. Power

Beebe Windmill (1820), Bridge-hampton, N.Y. (Chalmers G. Long, Jr., HAER)

Union Stock Yards Gate (1870s, Burnham and Root), Chicago. Oc-cupying more than one square mile, the yards were a city unto them-selves. (Chicago Historical Society)

Marshall Field and Company Wholesale House (1887, Henry Hobson Richardson), Chicago. (Chicago Historical Society)

or generating stations, sewage or water pumping stations and other utility buildings are highly visible and so tend to be architecturally refined. Power plants are easily identified by their large chimneys and vast coal piles. Their counterpart, the hydroelectric station, will, of course, be located above, below or near a dam, or connected to it by large penstocks (pipes). Such buildings invariably are of a single story and tall, to accommodate the overhead traveling crane necessary for initial assembly and later maintenance of the machinery.

The final type of industrial building is that in which the specialized nature of the process dictates a special form. Glass and ceramic factories built up to the early 20th century are easily identifiable by the upper part of the "bottle" kiln or glass "cone" projecting through the roof, while brick and tile works before 1940 usually burned their product in large cylindrical "beehive" ovens, themselves of brick, with low domed roofs. Perhaps the most distinctive function-specific structures are silos and elevators designed expressly for the storage of powdered and granular bulk products such as flour and cement.

From the standpoint of pure form, the most visually interesting industrial structures are those that cannot be termed buildings—the pure structures or complexes of

Grain elevator and mill, Petaluma, Calif. (Don Meacham)

Blast furnaces (1902–64), Sloss-Sheffield Steel and Iron Company, Birmingham, Ala. (James Y. Hunt; Jack E. Boucher, HAER)

apparatus that enclose no space, stand freely and exist for a single purpose, usually to process a bulk product. For example, blast furnaces, those tall cylindrical structures with their ganglia of large downcomer pipes, are starkly functional and expressive of their purpose in life.

The creators of industrial structures for the most part have been anonymous, evolving from general architects or, more commonly, the firm's own employees in the 19th century to a separate profession of consulting architects and engineers by mid-century, to specialist consultants or firms that manufactured the production equipment.

The most adaptable industrial structures are the least specialized enclosures of space—the small- and medium-sized factories and mills with reasonably low stories. These are being converted to an astonishing variety of uses, ranging from other industrial functions to housing and artists' studios. But other industrial structures can find a new, radically different life—such as the Quaker Oats silos (1910 and 1932) in Akron, converted to a hotel, or a large generating station (1904) in Baltimore that is being adapted as an indoor amusement park and shopping mall. An unused blast furnace or other highly specialized structure can rarely be saved, and then only if it is preserved on its own merits as a historic monument. ★

Gas holder (1872), Petersburg Gas Light Company, Petersburg, Va. (Jack E. Boucher, HABS)

Pig iron kiln near Escanaba, Mich., built of stone and brick and resembling a fortress. (Balthazar Korab)

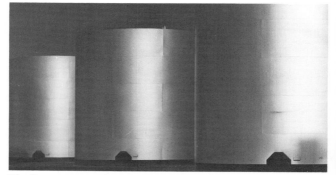

Oil refinery storage tanks, Baytown, Tex. (Russell Lee, University of Louisville Photographic Archives)

Ohio Steel Foundry Roll Shop (1939, Albert Kahn), Lima, Ohio, an International Style design. (Hedrich-Blessing)

Shoshone Hydroelectric Plant (1908–09), Garfield County, Colo., a significant engineering accomplishment because of its scale and the physical difficulties of construction. (Paul M. Murillo, HAER)

Wool carding machines, Merrimack Trading and Spinning Company (1830s), Lowell, Mass., a 19th-century textile factory. (© Randolph Langenbach)

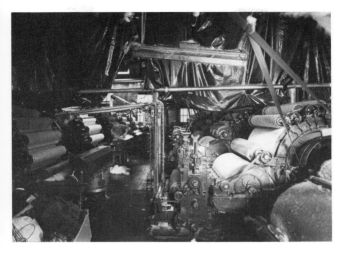

U.S. Steel limestone quarry, near Rogers City, Mich. (Balthazar Korab)

Occidental Mine, Comstock Historic District, Nev., with an adit, an almost horizontal entrance. (Martin Stupich)

LIBRARIES
George S. Bobinski

Libraries have been in existence since around 2000 B.C. and were evident in the United States from the early colonial period. The Redwood Library and Athenaeum (1748, Peter Harrison) in Newport, R.I., is the oldest library structure still dedicated to its original purpose. However, it was not until about 100 years ago that libraries began to be built in great numbers in separate buildings. Andrew Carnegie stimulated library development through his funding of 1,679 public library buildings in 1,412 communities as well as 108 academic library buildings, primarily during the period 1897–1917. Of the approximately 15,000 library buildings in the United States, half have been built since World War II.

Library building design is influenced by the need to house a collection of books and other information materials and provide seating and study facilities as well as work space for staff. Before World War II libraries tended to be of monumental character and in whatever architectural style was in favor. Major examples include the Beaux-Arts Library of Congress (1897, Smithmeyer and Pelz) and the classical New York Public Library (1911, Carrère and Hastings). Such early library buildings tended to be overly decorative as well as unexpandable, with little attention paid to function.

During the early 1930s architect Edward Tilton planned an open and flexible public library building at Springfield, Mass., that could be entered at the sidewalk level. Important public library buildings in Baltimore (1933, Edward L. Tilton and Alfred M. Githins) and Toledo (1940, Hahn and Hayes) followed the same form. During the same period architect-turned-bookstack-manufacturer Angus Snead Macdonald widely advocated a freer, more open approach to library planning with less dependence on fixed, load-bearing stacks and walls. Librarian Ralph Ellsworth was instrumental in having his new library building at Iowa State University (1947, Keffer and Jones) follow these principles.

By about 1950 library buildings began to be modular, flexible and open and inviting in design for users. They no longer looked alike, as each tended to have its own

Redwood Library (1748, Peter Harrison), Newport, R.I. (Cervin Robinson, HABS)

Riggs Library (1889–91) in Healy
Hall (1877–79, Smithmeyer and
Pelz), Georgetown University, Wash-
ington, D.C. (Walter Smalling, Jr.)

Library of Congress (1897,
Smithmeyer and Pelz), Washington,
D.C., one of America's most gran-
diose Beaux-Arts designs with a
magificent reading room. (Library of
Congress; Jack E. Boucher, HABS)

original style. The Washington University Library (1962, Murphy and Mackey, Inc.) in St. Louis exemplifies a library with an exterior design that evolved from the demands of the interior functions. Libraries could now be easily rearranged or expanded. The involvement of librarians in the planning process was an important element in these changes. The period 1950–75 marked the golden age of library expansion in the United States.

Even though the tempo of library building has lessened in the last 10 years because of economic factors, the open, inviting and flexible style and other innovations have continued. Increasing emphasis has been placed on energy conservation, removal of architectural barriers for the handicapped and adaptation to new computer technology and nonprint media.

A recent trend has been the conversion of vacant buildings in some communities to public libraries, such as the use of the 1912 Goldblatt Department Store as a new central building for the Chicago Public Library. Some older libraries, such as the Athenaeum in Providence, R.I., have been renovated or had additions built. Many of the Carnegie libraries are also being preserved, usually with interior renovation as well as building additions. ★

Newberry Library (1892, Henry Ives Cobb), Chicago, a massive Renaissance-style structure incorporating an innovative stack design. (Chicago Historical Society)

Low Memorial Library (1897, McKim, Mead and White), Columbia University, New York City, a Beaux-Arts building. (Columbiana Collection, Columbia University)

Carnegie Library (1913, William Sidney Pitman), Houston. (Houston Public Library)

North Manchester Public Library (1911), North Manchester, Ind. (P. D. Adams, HABS)

Los Angeles Public Library (1925, Bertram Goodhue). (HABS)

San Juan Capistrano Public Library (1983, Michael Graves), San Juan Capistrano, Calif., a postmodern library recalling the region's Spanish colonial history. (Proto Acme)

LIGHTHOUSES
F. Ross Holland, Jr.

A lighthouse has one main function: to provide a platform for a light by which mariners can navigate. Lighthouse builders learned early that flat sides receive the full force of a storm, but a round light tower breaks the forces of the sea and wind. Thus, most lighthouses are round.

Light towers on the East Coast are generally tall because the land is low and the height is needed to raise the light to a proper altitude so that vessels can see it. Light towers on the West Coast, however, are usually short because their sites are often several hundred feet above sea level. A harbor light does not have to be seen at great distances; consequently, these towers are short. Some light towers on the Gulf Coast and the Great Lakes are tall but most are of medium height.

Over the years, three types of lighthouses have been built in this country: the masonry tower, the screwpile lighthouse and the caisson lighthouse. Masonry towers have been made of fieldstone, granite and brick. They are, with only rare exception, simple conical structures, and any distinctive architectural embellishments are usually limited to the entrance way.

Screwpile lighthouses, whose design was imported from England in the 1850s, were used in bays, rivers and harbors. These lighthouses had giant screws, which were twisted into the sandy bottom and supported metal legs. The legs, held together with braces, formed the foundation of the lighthouse. An octagonal dwelling rested on the foundation system, and the light surmounted the one-story dwelling. Examples of this type can be found at the Chesapeake Bay Maritime Museum, St. Michaels, Md., and the Calvert Marine Museum, Solomons, Md. Ironpile lighthouses, an immediate predecessor of the screwpile type, were used on the Florida coast and were placed in the ocean. Being coastal lights, they were much taller. The dwelling and storage area was placed about halfway up the skeletal tower, which narrowed as it rose into the air; on the top perched the lantern with its light, consisting of a Fresnal lens.

Portland Head Light (1787–90) and keeper's house (1891), Cape Elizabeth, Maine. An early federal project, the tower survives essentially as constructed with some interior modifications. (Jack E. Boucher, HABS)

The caisson lighthouse succeeded the screwpile structure in Chesapeake Bay and bays further north. Because more ice was encountered in these bays and harbors, the Lighthouse Service found it difficult to devise adequate barriers to protect the screwpile lighthouses. The caisson structure consisted of a huge iron tube that was towed to the desired site and dropped into the water upright. The workers leveled the tube on the bottom and then filled it with rubble and concrete. On this foundation the dwelling was erected and the light placed on top.

The dwellings at light stations reflected current architectural styles of the period or the local architecture and were highly varied. For example, a quaint Second Empire dwelling with a tower was built at Fort Tompkins on Staten Island, N.Y. Many of the dwellings at southern lighthouses were board-and-batten structures typical of that coastal section. On the West Coast all the early dwellings were Cape Cod in style, because when the first light stations were established there in the 1850s, the building plans were prepared in Washington, D.C. The Point Pinos lighthouse in Monterey, Calif., is typical of this style.

Lighthouses are painted with distinctive colors and markings. The Fire Island, N.Y., lighthouse had alternate wide black and white bands, for example, and the Cape Hatteras, N.C., lighthouse has spiral banding. These markings made them good daymarks to aid navigators in determining their position.

For many years, light towers had to be substantial structures and enclosed to protect the light, which was fire in some form (such as candles and lamps), from wind and rain. Today, lighthouse lights are electric, and the lamps or bulbs are sealed from the weather. Consequently, only a strong, simple structure, such as a steel skeleton tower, is needed to support the light. In some instances when a lighthouse became automatic, the light was moved to such a structure at the station. ★

Portland Breakwater Lighthouse (1855, 1875), South Portland, Maine, a small classical structure made of cast iron. (Gerda Peterich, HABS)

Point Loma Lighthouse (1855), San Diego, Calif., a station atop the keeper's house. (Edward Sievers, San Diego–California Club)

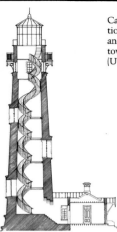

Pigeon Point Lighthouse (1871–72), San Mateo, Calif., a sectional drawing showing the staircase. (HABS)

Cape Hatteras Light Station (1871), N.C., a black-and-white spiral banded tower with a brick base. (U.S. Coast Guard)

Opposite: Thomas Point Lighthouse (1875), Thomas Point, Md., a hexagonal screwpile lighthouse. (C. C. Harris, Chesapeake Bay Maritime Museum)

Liston Range Rear Light (1876–77), Biddles Corner, Del., a wrought-iron range light on the Delaware River. (George Rineer, Eleutherian Mills-Hagley Foundation, HAER)

Alcatraz Light Station (1854), Alcatraz Island, Calif., an octagonal tower that is the oldest light on the Pacific coast. (U.S. Coast Guard)

MAIN STREETS
Richard Longstreth

Main Street has long been used as a generic term to identify the principal corridor of small cities and towns throughout the United States. While linear settlement forms date from the initial period of Anglo-American colonization and much earlier abroad, the concept of Main Street stems from the emergence of distinct functional zones in the development of communities during the 19th and first half of the 20th centuries. Many of these communities were planned, that is, built according to a predetermined street layout, and that plan more often than not took the form of an orthogonal grid. Unto itself, the grid is neutral with few, if any, blocks differing from one another. Yet, an interplay of economic and civic factors contributed to concentrating important activities along or near one street, which became an emblem of the community's progress as well as the major thoroughfare.

In general terms, Main Street provided the focus for retailing, with the most prestigious businesses tending to congregate at the center. Banks located there, as did the more respectable hotels. Main Street also harbored public buildings, fraternal organizations, theaters and other centers of community life. Churches were often situated toward the periphery of this core. Further out at one or both ends, the street might be lined with a number of elaborate residences and perhaps the high school and other education facilities.

Several variations on this diagrammatic model exist. In a number of towns, notably those planned in conjunction with railroad lines, there are two main streets. One, paralleling the tracks, is defined by businesses and light industry. The other, intersecting at right angles at the center, tends to be the spine for public and institutional buildings as well as the better residential precincts. Many communities, especially in parts of the South and Midwest, have a central square, usually containing a courthouse, with institutional and commercial buildings

around it. The larger the settlement, the greater the likelihood of those functions occupying an area several blocks wide; however, one street almost always remains dominant.

Size can also be a primary determinant of Main Street's appearance. Communities that became large towns or small cities by the early 20th century often contain one or more tall buildings (generally banks or hotels) near the center and have other more elaborate edifices as well. In the smallest towns, particularly in the Midwest and West, one-story buildings may predominate, many of them freestanding. Otherwise, the form and scale of most commercial districts are relatively homogeneous, with buildings with two to three and seldom more than four stories abutting one another, their street elevations defining the property's edge. More often than not, building facades adhere to one of a few basic compositional patterns that were used nationwide. However, they may vary considerably in detail according to factors such as the building's function, when the community was settled, the periods in which it was prosperous and the sophistication of the designers. Until recent years, trees seldom existed in the commercial center except in squares and parks or as adornment for public buildings. Residential quarters provide a sharp contrast, with most buildings set back on generously landscaped tracts. Here, too, the street is usually lined with large trees, accentuating the change from the outskirts on one side and the community core on the other.

As a place, Main Street represents far more than a locus of businesses and fine houses. It is a center for informal socializing and special events, for private display and public ceremony, a symbol of achievement and potential. Although this multifaceted role has eroded in numerous instances over the past several decades, it remains strong in many others and of late is enjoying regeneration. ★

Harrison Avenue, Guthrie, Okla., c. 1900, lined by typical early western false-front buildings. (Oklahoma Historical Society)

Main Street, Minot, N.D., c. 1910, with well-developed Italianate brick shops framing a broad avenue. (State Historical Society of Wisconsin)

Main Street, Springfield, Mass., c. 1908, where trolleys brought shoppers and workers to new high-rises downtown. (William Henry Jackson, HABS)

Main Street architecture, Selma, Ala., 1935, reflecting the expressive qualities of Italianate building elements and materials. (Walker Evans, FSA/OWI)

S. D. Morgan and Company Building (J. S. Reeves and Company Building) (c. 1875), Nashville, showing the tripartite structure of most Main Street buildings—shopfront, upper stories and cornice. (Robert J. Dunay, HABS)

Main Street commercial block, Madison, Ind., where merchants have rehabilitated stores and improved added signage such as this. (Balthazar Korab)

Main Street, Cascade, Iowa, 1937, with neon signage typical of the period. (Russell Lee, Library of Congress)

Main Street, Tarboro, N.C., where a three-year pilot program of downtown revitalization, historic preservation and economic development has been undertaken. (Tom Lutz, National Main Street Center)

Mulberry Street block, Madison, Ind., showing a homogeneity resulting from similar scales and heights as well as diverse styles. (H. T. Moriarity, HABS)

MARKETS
Padraic Burke

The act of going to the marketplace is one of the most basic social functions. How and where we shop for what we eat tells a great deal about our culture and society. In the medieval city, the market was often found at the most important intersection in town. Usually it was adjacent to or attached to the church. As the market street grew into the market square, it began to take on a variety of shapes and forms. Sometimes it was affixed to neighboring houses or the church and at other times it led into lesser and subordinate squares.

The most important element of the market was its public character. Administered by a public agency, it existed to serve a variety of public needs, from court to meeting place. The economic foundation on which the public market rested was an egalitarian one that guaranteed access to all producers. In the United States, the enforcement of market regulations was handled by a market master; every market, including those in Boston and Philadelphia, possessed a pillory.

Just when the medieval market was losing much of its public character in Europe in the early 17th century, it took root in the emerging villages and towns of North America. In communities whose locus and focus lay between the meetinghouse and town hall, the public market occupied a central position. By 1690 the major colonial towns (Boston, Philadelphia, New York, Charleston, S.C., and Newport, R.I.) held weekly markets at a given time and place and under regulated conditions. In 1633–34 Boston became the first colonial town to establish a public market. By 1658 Boston's public market occupied the bottom half of a new two-story building, with the town hall above. Primarily a market, it also served as a town hall, courthouse, meeting place, library, armory and commercial center.

By the beginning of the 18th century, New York City had seven public markets and Philadelphia had a model market (1710) that inspired imitations in such cities as Lexington, Ky., Louisville, Cincinnati and Pittsburgh. Throughout the century, Philadelphia's market was one of the most vital institutions in the city, and its most important thoroughfare was renamed Market Street after the building that dominated the physical and social

Interior, High Street Market (1710), Philadelphia. (William Birch, Free Library of Philadelphia)

Opposite: New Market (1745), Philadelphia, an open market with a gabled roof built in imitation of European country markets. (William Birch and Son, Historical Society of Pennsylvania)

environment. The sturdy, somewhat shedlike structure had a gabled roof supported by brick piers; its upper chambers also housed the office of the Pennsylvania colony. The market was soon incapable of handling the throngs of farmers and shoppers, so stalls were erected on neighboring streets; by the mid-1770s sheds extended for several blocks.

In the eastern United States the predominant building type was a rectangular brick shed, several bays in length and about one and one-half stories in height. On the West Coast, the predominant type was a rambling affair composed of both permanent market buildings and the common open shed with a roof.

The economic and social vitality of the urban public market has declined considerably in the last 50 years. Traditionally served by small farms on the edges of the city, markets were made obsolescent by the growth of large-scale mechanized farming and improved transportation and refrigeration. The rise of the supermarket beginning in the 1930s also made heavy inroads into the economic vitality of the market.

A resurgence of public markets began in the 1960s. Some cities realized the traditional importance of the market in urban design and have sought to reestablish them in downtown public squares. Other markets have been saved and revitalized for continued use as markets or adapted to new purposes. In Boston Quincy Market (1826) was reborn in 1976 as Faneuil Hall Marketplace with a mix of markets and boutiques that has spawned similar recycled marketplaces throughout the country. The sprawling and vigorous Pike Place Market (1907) in Seattle was spared from urban renewal and made the centerpiece of a historic district with the help of a voters' referendum.

What gives the public market its unique character is that it is a living institution where people buy real and essential things. The market is the ideal place for natural rhythm within the built environment. And it is not a metaphor for life, but life itself. ★

Interior of a California meat market, c. 1890. (Grahame H. Hardy)

South Water Street Market, Chicago, c. 1900. Farmers sold their produce from wagons and carts. (Chicago Historical Society)

Indianapolis City Market (Market House) (1886, D. A. Bohlen), Indianapolis, a brick structure incorporating Richardsonian Romanesque elements. The roof is supported by iron trussing. (Jack E. Boucher, HABS)

French Market (Old Vegetable Market) (1822, Joseph Pilie), New Orleans, a stuccoed brick building with three rows of Doric columns running the length of the wings. (Historic New Orleans Collection)

Quincy Market (1825–26, Alexander Parris), Boston, a three-building complex converted into Faneuil Hall Marketplace. (David Cubbage)

Pike Place Market (1907–17), Seattle, an active farmers market saved through a historic district ordinance. (Nick Jahn)

PRISONS
Robert B. MacKay

The young American republic's first great contribution to world architectural thought was, as architectural historian Henry-Russell Hitchcock has observed, "strictly social and organizational." It was the novel design of our jails and prisons that first attracted interest from abroad.

Within a few decades after the Revolution, Philadelphia's Quaker activists had succeeded in establishing incarceration as an alternative to the primary instrument of the English penal code they so abhorred—corporal punishment. Under the Pennsylvania System, prisoners were left to their reflections in solitary cellular confinement until they achieved penitence, root of the word "penitentiary." As early as 1790, solitary cells had been added to Philadelphia's Walnut Street Jail, a typical colonial jail, where convicts of every description intermingled in large rooms.

However, it was English emigré architect John Haviland's Eastern Penitentiary (1823–29) in Philadelphia that was to introduce cellular construction on a large scale and popularize radial planning for penitentiaries. General Lafayette visited Eastern, as did Dickens, who called it one of the two sites he most wanted to see in America, and de Toqueville, who came to America as a member of the French penal commission. Haviland went on to perfect his radial penitentiary plan at the New Jersey State Prison (1833–36) in Trenton, which became the most copied correctional design of the 19th century. Versions of this prison can be found across Europe, as well as in Russia, Japan and South America.

Europeans were also interested in the Virginia State Prison (1797–1800), a U-shaped cellular prison based on Englishman Jeremy Bentham's circular Panopticon principle; the Egyptian Revival Halls of Justice in New York City, a high-rise cellular prison designed by Haviland and labeled "The Tombs" by the press; and Sing Sing, the huge, thousand-cell prison on the Hudson River above Manhattan, to which inmates had to be "sent up the river." Sing Sing (1825) was actually built for a variant program of cellular confinement known as the Auburn System, in which inmates worked together during the daylight hours and were placed in solitary cells at night. The chief architectural feature of the Auburn System was the inside cell block, where tiers of cells were placed back to back with air space between the cell block and the outer walls. Gridley J. F. Bryant and Louis Dwight

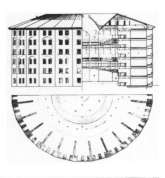

Opposite: Newgate Prison (c. 1650), Newgate, Conn., a complex including a guard room, workshop, bake house, coal house and well. (Connecticut Historical Society)

Panopticon plan (1790, Jeremy Bentham). Although never built in Bentham's lifetime, it was the prototype for many later prisons. (Jeremy Bentham, *Works*)

Eastern State Penitentiary (1823–29, John Haviland), a massive radial-plan Gothic Revival structure that became an international model. (NTHP Collection)

succeeded in adapting the Auburn cell block to a radial plan—the cruciform—at Boston's Charles Street Jail (1848–51), which had a greater influence on American prison design during the second half of the 19th century than Haviland's plans. Charles Street was also the first realized American plan to be published in the important London architectural periodical, *The Builder*, in 1849.

A third type of prison configuration used in America in the early decades of the 20th century was the "telephone pole" plan, where wings were built at right angles to a central corridor. The telephone pole was a French concept, thought to have been popularized in this country by prison architect Alfred Hopkins, who used it for the federal penitentiary at Lewisburg, Pa., in 1932.

Because new prisons are usually a low priority for governments, most architectural firms rarely get a chance to design new facilities and tend to turn to existing solutions. H. H. Richardson, for example, copied Bryant's Charles Street Jail for his 1884 jail within the Allegheny County Courthouse and Jail in Pittsburgh, while one of America's largest 20th-century state prisons, the Illinois State Penitentiary (1916–24) near Joliet, is a throwback to Bentham's Panopticon, featuring huge doughnut-shaped cell houses.

Prisons can present difficult adaptive use problems. Cell blocks are not easily removed. An 1884 county jail in Billings, Mont., is now the Yellowstone Art Center. Other prisons have found new lives as restaurants and even book depositories. Until 1976 Old Windsor Village, a 76-unit apartment complex overlooking Vermont's Green Mountains, served as the state prison. Among the new residents is a former guard. ★

Charles Street Jail (1848–51, Gridley J. F. Bryant and Louis Dwight), Boston, a radial plan. (Joseph Adams)

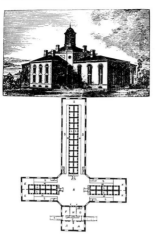

Halls of Justice and House of Detention (The Tombs) (1835–38, John Haviland), New York City, an Egyptian Revival prison. (RIBA)

Debtor's Wing of the Philadelphia County (Moyamensing) Prison (1832, Thomas U. Walter), Philadelphia, whose Egyptian Revival design was based on recent archeological discoveries. (Jack E. Boucher, HABS)

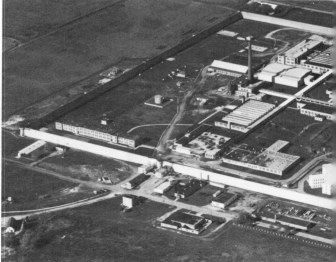

Allegheny County Jail (1884–88, Henry Hobson Richardson), Pittsburgh, a late and influential design of Richardson. (Houghton Library, Harvard University)

Interior, Baltimore City Jail (1859, Thomas and James M. Dixon), Baltimore. (Lanny Miyamoto, HABS)

Illinois State Penitentiary (1916–24), near Joliet, with its circular cell houses recalling the 18th-century Panopticon plan. (Illinois Department of Corrections)

Point of Rocks (Baltimore and
Ohio) Railroad Station (1870s, at-
tributed to E. Francis Baldwin),
Point of Rocks, Md., a picturesque
High Victorian Gothic suburban
station. (Wm. Edmund Barrett,
HAER)

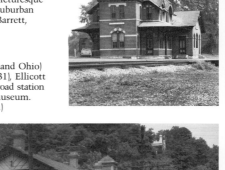

Ellicott City (Baltimore and Ohio)
Railroad Station (1830–31), Ellicott
City, Md., the oldest railroad station
in the country, now a museum.
(Herbert H. Harwood, Jr.)

Mt. Airy (Reading Company) Railroad Station (1883, Frank Furness),
Mt. Airy, Pa., a Stick Style structure, one of several stations designed by Furness in the
Philadelphia area. (Herbert H.
Harwood, Jr.)

Interior of an Amtrak waiting
room, Michigan. (Balthazar Korab)

RAILROAD STATIONS
Herbert H. Harwood, Jr.

They were railroad—never "train"—stations. During the height of the railroad era, the station was a major community commercial and social center.

The first U.S. common carrier railroad ran in 1830; others appeared quickly and grew in length. The first priority was to build track, then freight-handling facilities, so in many cases the "station" was merely a room in some adjacent inn or tavern. But growing traffic volumes demanded more space, better outdoor shelter and a layout that could efficiently handle the separate flows of people, parcels and package freight—all of which dictated a design different from any existing architecture. By the late 1830s, an almost universal pattern had been developed for the next hundred years.

The essential internal components were one or perhaps two passenger waiting rooms, one or two rooms for baggage, express and small-lot freight, and an agent's office. The agent's office was centrally situated; it also generally included a projecting track-side bay so he could easily see train movements. Externally, the station was distinguished by its agent's bay and, usually, train order signals. But its most unmistakable architectural ingredient was a wide overhanging roof at first-floor level, suitable for sheltering waiting passengers and working railroaders, and supported by impressive brackets. For larger stations with multiple tracks, platform sheds or a single large train shed covering the whole track area was added.

Around these basic elements grew an awesome array of architectural treatments and construction materials. Well over 80,000 U.S. stations were built, most during the railroad construction frenzy in the late 19th century. The majority were simple standardized frame structures stamped out by each railroad's engineering department. The "typical" smaller station was one story, although many included second-floor living quarters for the agent or, at crew change points, operating offices.

At larger volume points designs became more elaborate and permanent, often expressing corporate egos or community pride. Typically, a town started with a standard wood combination passenger and freight station; as it prospered, the freight was exiled to a separate warehouse-style depot and a commodious brick or stone structure arose for passengers—often with a clock tower, dominating the town center. Big-city terminals developed into their own specialized, and usually monumental, breed, often designed by nationally notable architects in styles suitable for grand civic structures, which after the 1893 World's Columbian Exposition usually meant Beaux-Arts or Classical Revival.

Suburban points, which began developing in the 1870s and 1880s, got the most consistently careful architectural attention, because the station was an integral part of the rarefied residential community it created. Locally prominent architects often were called on for these. Elsewhere, stations followed whatever residential architectural style was fashionable in their time.

Rapidly declining passenger traffic, escalating property taxes and deteriorating railroad finances triggered whole-

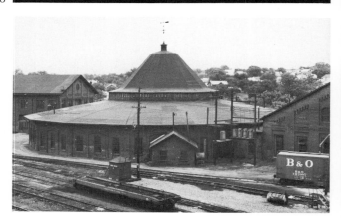

Baltimore and Ohio Railroad Roundhouse, Martinsburg, W. Va. (Wm. Edmund Barrett, HAER)

Rock Island Railroad Roundhouse, El Reno, Okla. (Charles Rotkin, Standard Oil of New Jersey Collection)

Shed and tracks, Chicago and Northwestern Railway Company Station (1882), Chicago. (Chicago Historical Society)

Two types of train shed roof trusses. (David Weitzman, *Traces of the Past: A Field Guide to Industrial Archaeology*)

sale station closings starting in the early 1950s. Since then, mechanization and centralization of agency functions are finishing the process. The large urban terminals are special problems. These sit on highly valuable downtown property, but tend to be defiant space-wasters—low-rise buildings with vast concourses and waiting rooms, designed in ways difficult to adapt to practical uses. But, happily, their flexible design, sturdy construction and historical importance have saved many smaller stations for other uses—homes, stores, banks, restaurants, libraries, community centers and even railroad services. ★

Above and right: Pennsylvania Station (1906–10, McKim, Mead and White), New York City, a now-demolished grand station based on the Baths of Caracalla with a monumental steel and glass concourse. (Pennsylvania Railroad; Cervin Robinson, HABS)

Above: Grand Central Terminal (1903–13, Reed and Stem; Warren and Wetmore), New York City, a surviving Beaux-Arts landmark. (Municipal Archives of the City of New York; Ed Nowak)

St. Louis Union Station (1892–94, Theodore C. Link and Edward A. Cameron), St. Louis, typical of the larger Richardsonian Romanesque stations of the period. (Arteaga)

Los Angeles Union Station (1938, John and Donald Parkinson and Herman Sacks), Los Angeles, reflecting the city's Spanish colonial heritage. (Union Pacific Railroad)

Orlando Train Station (1926), Orlando, Fla., with towers and round arches typical of the Spanish colonial revival. (John Parks, HABS)

Below and middle: Cincinnati Union Terminal (1933, Alfred Fellheimer and Steward Wagner), Cincinnati, an unusual Art Deco station whose mosaic murals depict Cincinnati and U.S. history. (Director of Public Utilities, Cincinnati)

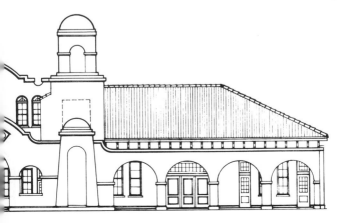

RANCHES
Alvin G. Davis

Ranching, as a way of life in the United States, was started in what is now the southwestern part of the country with the earliest missionary efforts. Hernando Cortez introduced Spanish horses and longhorn Andalusian cattle into the newly acquired conquered land in 1591. These animals adapted to the environment and multiplied into large herds of longhorn cattle and bands of mustangs. Both became fair game for anyone who could rope and brand them.

An agricultural industry was thus started that required buildings and equipment for housing and handling both people and livestock. Ranch architecture generally reflected the requirements imposed by functional needs, climate and, sometimes, the demands of defense, as well as indigenous materials that were available for construction.

Early ranching operations north of the Rio Grande were operated from the Spanish missions. Grazing lands were located some distance around the missions. A typical mission usually included living quarters, a chapel and a plaza surrounded by an enclosure with several bastions. At the same time, secular ranching started in outlying areas.

The Spanish ranchers built their ranches as compounds, enclosing several structures in addition to the main house: sheds for horses, goats and sheep; stalls for milk cows; and storage areas for hay. These structures served as protection against the weather and intruders who might steal the livestock. The earliest Anglo ranches had few, if any, outbuildings but did have corrals, made of log, adobe or stone, to keep their herds from straying. During the earliest stages of ranching, the outbuildings were constructed of whatever materials were available, just as the main houses were. The size, intended use and

Magnolia Ranch (Chesbro Ranch) (1883), near Winfield, Kans., a noteworthy complex of stone buildings that is still a working ranch. (Everts, *Atlas of Kansas, 1887,* Kansas State Historical Society)

materials dictated the style of the structures, which did not necessarily match that of the main house.

The main houses at the early Spanish ranches were consistent in style with the dwellings the ranchers had known in Mexico before emigrating. They were simple massive cubes with walls made of blocks of caliche or of sandstone quarried and dressed with hand tools. As ranching moved east, where native timber was available, the log cabin became a common ranch structure. In the northern hill country of Texas, combination stone and timber houses were common. A real luxury home for the period and location consisted of a double log cabin joined together by a dog trot (breezeway) with lean-to rooms of stone on the backs of the log cabins. In more desolate areas, ranchers created Sotol houses, built of the flowering stems of the sawtooth yucca that had been stripped and dried.

The western movement of ranching into the plains area brought about new types of architecture. One common form of ranch house was the half dugout, in which half of the single-story building was below ground level and half above. Another was the above-ground box-and-strip (board-and-batten) house. Such construction required milled lumber in its entirety, but a lesser quantity than studded walls would have. The extension of railroads had made the materials less expensive, but they still had to be freighted some distance. Stone was also used as the principal building material for ranch houses in some areas.

Many ranch houses evolved from simple structures, often one room. As families and fortunes grew, box-and-strip and other types of additions were made, creating sizable and comfortable homes that, in some instances, approached true elegance. The best architectural concepts represented by these houses have been continued and, in many cases, combined to create current ranch architecture. ★

Ed P. Steele Ranch, near Boulder, Wyo., encompassing frame buildings and a small corral nestled at the foot of the Rockies. (Richard Collier, Wyoming Recreation Commission)

Ranch house, Warner Ranch
(c. 1840), near San Diego, a way-
station for travelers on the Sante Fe
Trail. The buildings, typical of the
early West, are of adobe brick and
handhewn timbers. (James Pitts and
Bob Fong, HABS)

Box-and-strip (board-and-batten)
ranch house (c. 1903), moved from
west-central Texas to Lubbock.
(Alvin G. Davis)

Picket-and-sotol house (c. 1904), re-
located from Ozona to Lubbock,
Tex. (Alvin G. Davis)

Barton House (c. 1909), an elaborate
frame main house moved from the
Texas panhandle to Lubbock. (Alvin
G. Davis)

Grant-Kohrs Ranch (1863), Deer
Lodge, Mont., where registered
purebred cattle were first introduced into the state. (Jack E.
Boucher, HABS)

Cookhouse, Padlock Ranch, Mont., built of logs, wood and tin and located in a cow camp many miles from the ranch headquarters. (Dudley Witney)

Recreation hall, HF Bar Ranch, near Buffalo, Wyo., an unusual two-story log structure. (Richard Collier, Wyoming Recreation Commission)

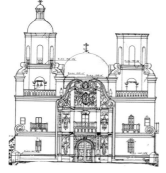

Opposite: San Estevan del Ray Mission Church (c. 1629–42), Acoma Pueblo, N.M., combining native materials, Indian building skills and Spanish baroque forms. (M. James Slack, HABS)

Mission San Xavier del Bac (1784–97), near Tucson, one of the great mission churches. The elaborate central entrance contrasts with the relatively plain surfaces of the towers. (William M. Collier, Jr., and Louis Williams, HABS)

Old Roman Catholic Cathedral (Minor Basilica) (1806–21, Benjamin H. Latrobe), Baltimore, the first Roman Catholic cathedral built in the United States. (Sandak, Inc.)

St. Michael's Episcopal Church (1752–61, attributed to Samuel Cardy), Charleston, S.C., a Georgian-style church with a typical Anglican steeple. (Mark W. Steele, HABS)

St. Luke's Church (1632), near Smithfield, Va., with hallmarks of the English Gothic parish church—tower, steep roof, buttresses and lancet-arched windows. (John O. Bostrup, HABS)

RELIGIOUS ARCHITECTURE
Phoebe Stanton

"Our churches are the petrifaction of our religion," wrote Samuel Taylor Coleridge in 1818. Religious architecture has, throughout history and in a variety of cultures, expressed its function in its form. It has been molded around the ceremony of belief. The earliest Christian churches are described as having assumed "the shape of the liturgy"; the interior, either rectangular or round, focused the attention of the laity on a richly appointed altar, site of the mass.

Perpetuation of tradition is a function of religious buildings. The forms of interior spaces and the character of the architecture that surrounds them have been perceived as precious because they are illustrative of the history of faith. Changes in the liturgy and the social role of churches, in their wealth and the number and kind of their members and in the society of which they were a part have caused development of traditional architectural forms rather than the invention of new ones. Preaching orders and Protestant communities, because they required verbal communication, for example, kept the style of architecture with which they were familiar but adapted it to halls in which sermons could be heard.

The size and decoration of churches also express function. Churches frequently contain treasures of the decorative arts. They may be austere. Both approaches reveal the nature of belief. Because they are consecrated structures, churches and their treasures have tended to survive. Rich or modest, they bespeak the life and religious values of the society they served.

Early religious architecture in the United States functioned well because it continued traditions brought by the colonists from their homelands. The English late Gothic village church was familiar to craftsman and worshiper. Congregational communities in New England arranged the interior space in their wooden churches to focus attention on the pulpit and the preacher yet used English late medieval vernacular carpentry. In the West, the Spanish baroque style survived, although it was radically simplified through the use of adobe.

Eighteenth-century churches continued to follow foreign models. Because the colonists in the East felt allied with English culture, their growing urban communities built adaptations of churches by Christopher Wren and James Gibbs. With greater wealth, a richer baroque style developed in the West.

At the end of the century, with the revival of the classical and Gothic styles, a change occurred in English and American religious architecture. Perpetuation of tradition was both less and more important. Classical buildings, associated with Roman Christian architecture, addressed contemporary life and secular values. The use of the Gothic style, the preeminent European Christian style, consciously emphasized the history of the church. Both styles offered opportunities for innovation. The classical was at first victorious, producing inventive buildings, while the Gothic satisfied a desire for ritual and the richness of tradition.

In the late 19th and early 20th centuries, an infinite number of expressions of revival styles developed. The wealth of congregations and the history of their beliefs were expressed in the style and ornamentation of church buildings. The Episcopal church tended to adopt the English Gothic style and to experiment with the Romanesque. Other Protestant and Catholic communities employed medieval styles but in a less English form. Other faiths used styles associated with their origins; synagogues and Eastern and Greek Orthodox churches accepted Byzantine inspiration. New denominations, such as the Church of Christ, Scientist, tended to adopt a classical style.

In the 20th century, design alternatives have included modification of the interior plan, the use of styles not

Frame churches, near Winner, S.D., 1938, creating a uniquely American scene. (Dorothea Lange, Oakland Museum)

historically associated with Christianity, the legible expression of symbols of the faith and attempts to build exactly in medieval styles, as at the National Cathedral in Washington, D.C. Experimentation with plans has occurred in response to new requirements and because congregations are adventurous or are convinced that the history of worship suggests it. Some architects have kept the traditional form of space but surrounded it with a nontraditional building.

The inherent conservatism of religious communities and the place of religion in contemporary life explain why church architecture, in a period in which architects have stressed an aesthetic of functional statement, has inevitably been comparatively less important than secular building. At the same time, ministry by television, the establishment of new residential communities and a need for buildings for social activities—which now play so large a part in the work of churches—are creating demands for which there are no historic stylistic patterns. New churches are becoming less traditional in form; they may refer indirectly to historic styles but their principal source of design is the life and needs of the communities they serve.

While many religious buildings survive and are in use, others have been abandoned or threatened by dwindling congregations caused by population shifts and social and economic changes. The cost of maintenance and restoration as well as the desire for more flexible facilities sometimes become obstacles to preservation. But imaginative alternative uses that respect the history of religious buildings are being found as a means of saving them. ★

Holy Trinity Russian Orthodox Cathedral and parish house (1903, Louis Sullivan), Chicago. (Chicago Historical Society)

Eldridge Street Synagogue (1887, Herter Brothers), New York City, with the intricate surface ornament and minaretlike spires characteristic of the Moorish Revival. (ASID)

Christian Science Church (1920, Irving J. Gill), San Diego, a modern design suggesting California's mission architecture. (Title Insurance and Trust Company Collection)

Unity Church (1906, Frank Lloyd Wright), Oak Park, Ill., whose exterior walls were cast in poured concrete with exposed pebble aggregate. (© Frank Lloyd Wright Foundation)

Kukui Shrine, Honolulu, a wooden shrine reflecting the Oriental presence in the islands. (Jack E. Boucher, HABS)

Garden Grove Community Church
(Crystal Cathedral) (1980, Johnson/
Burgee Architects), Garden Grove,
Calif., a dramatic contemporary
church made of glass and
white-painted steel.
(Gordon H. Schenck, Jr.)

St. Matthew's Church (1983, Moore Ruble Yudell), Pacific Palisades, Calif.,
a glass, wood and stucco structure with seating in the round to create a
sense of intimacy. (Timothy Hursley, Moore Ruble Yudell)

RESORT HOTELS
Jeffrey W. Limerick

Resort hotels provide a setting for rest and renewed health and the making of social contacts, business deals and every sort of amusement. Since colonial days, those who could afford the time and expense have gone to resort hotels near the shore, in the unspoiled countryside or near mineral springs and spas.

Hotels are, first and foremost, commercial enterprises whose primary purpose is to make money; art and lofty ideals have little to do with their design. They must efficiently and unobtrusively provide the services their patrons demand and, more important, a pleasant setting and atmosphere. As "nonserious," low-art architecture, these buildings are allowed the license to exaggerate.

The first hotels appeared in Europe in the late 1700s, when large rooms specifically for socializing, dining and entertainment were added to traditional inns. Early American inns followed suit. Dining, drinking, socializing and all the activities associated with the office or lobby took place in one or two large downstairs rooms. The guests shared whatever the landlord was having for dinner and slept upstairs in large common bedrooms. Sanitary facilities were in the stableyard. Washing up was done at the kitchen pump or well.

With the building of the Tremont House (1822, Isaiah Rogers) in Boston, Americans became leaders in hotel construction and innovation. This hotel featured the world's first lobby, indoor plumbing, a tasteful garden (instead of a stableyard) and private guest rooms with lockable doors. The Tremont established the arenas for competition among hotels that have lasted to the present: size, fashionable styling and decor, and the latest in technical and convenience gadgetry. Hotels have exposed the American public to new inventions before they became commonly available: the elevator, steam heating, modern indoor plumbing and improved fireproof and high-rise construction techniques, as well as box springs, the

Casino and Sea Beach Hotel (c. 1904), Santa Cruz, Calif., whose exotic style enhanced guests' sense of fantasy. (Library of Congress)

Opposite: Marlborough-Blenheim Hotel (1906, Price and McLanahan), on the boardwalk, Atlantic City, N.J.

Tremont House (1822, Isaiah
Rogers), Boston. (Society for the
Preservation of New England
Antiquities)

Hotel Del Coronado (1887–88,
James and Merritt Reid), San Diego,
a sprawling Queen Anne–style
hotel. (Rand McNally Company)

Traymore Hotel (1907, Price and McLanahan), Atlantic City, N.J., a grand hotel replaced by a casino. (Jack E. Boucher, HABS)

Colonial Hotel (1894–95), Cape May, N.J. (Jay Bargmann, HABS)

Awahnee Inn (1925–27, Gilbert Stanley Underwood), Yosemite National Park, Calif., in its majestic mountain setting. (Carleton Knight III)

waterbed, the electric light, the telephone, radio and television.

The modern hotel of the Tremont type began to appear at American resorts in the 1840s. Unlike city hotels, which were forced to build even higher because of high urban land costs, resort hotels tended to spread out in long wings with public rooms on the bottom floor and guest rooms along double-loaded corridors on several floors above. They were sited to monopolize the view of their particular attraction.

The expansion of the railroads after the Civil War greatly expanded the resort business. The railroads often built hotels at attractive spots along their lines to stimulate travel and investment in their nearby real estate holdings. Resorts of this period clothed themselves in stylized regional dress—for example, English and Spanish colonial styles—to attract patrons.

After World War I, hotels became even more stylized to evoke historical and exotic settings, yet with all the modern conveniences their clients expected. With the coming of the International Style in the 1930s and 1940s,

Mission Inn (1902–03, Arthur B. Benton), Riverside, Calif., an eclectic Spanish colonial revival design. (Jim Edwards)

Lobby, Old Faithful Inn (1902–03, Robert C. Reamer), Yellowstone National Park, Wyo., an architectural expression of its rustic surroundings, featuring a monumental stone fireplace and tree-branch balconies. (Library of Congress)

Grand Hotel (1887), Mackinac Island, Mich., a rambling Queen Anne–style hotel. (Balthazar Korab)

such overt historical imagery was regarded as wrong. Some designers found a compromise in the jazzy streamlined modernism of the Moderne or Art Deco. By the late 1940s, even this was regarded as falsely modern. Designers began to employ novel structural forms and decorative materials to create a wholly modern mood. The premier resort hotel of the early 1950s was Morris Lapidus's Fontainebleau in Miami Beach—the epitome of nouveau riche resort life.

With the passing of the International Style, architects are once again striving for greater drama, often drawing on overtly theatrical imagery. Many older hotels, like Atlantic City's famous Traymore, prove too expensive to run or repair and are torn down. Others have survived by being adapted to new uses as condominiums or offices. Still others, like the Broadmoor Hotel in Colorado Springs or the Grand Hotel on Mackinac Island, continue to enjoy steady popularity and, despite careful insertion of modern conveniences, manage to look much as they did when new, perpetuating the illusion that they exist solely for the individual guest's personal enjoyment. ★

ROW HOUSES
Charles Lockwood

Before the Revolution, most American city residents lived in freestanding houses surrounded by gardens or in small individually built dwellings that haphazardly lined the narrow winding streets. By the late 18th century, groups of uniform attached houses—or row houses—appeared in the largest cities, such as Boston, Providence, New York and Philadelphia. Within several decades, the row house had become the usual urban dwelling for all but the richest city residents, who could still afford a detached home and grounds, or the poorest, who lived several families to a run-down building in the oldest part of town or in shacks on the outskirts.

The row house achieved this near-universal popularity because attached dwellings made the best use of land in the densely populated early 19th-century cities where residents moved around on foot or by slow-moving omnibuses. Moreover, constructing a row of identical houses at once offered considerable economies of scale over singly built residences.

As architectural fashions changed from the Federal to the Greek Revival to the Italianate between the Revolution and the Civil War, American row houses reflected the latest styles in facade features such as the front door, ironwork or roofline and with interior ornament such as fireplace mantels and ceiling plasterwork. The facades fit the local taste and materials—such as brownstone in New York and Brooklyn, red brick in Boston and Baltimore and frame in San Francisco.

Over the decades, row house interior plans were quite similar, if only because of the narrow rectangular shape of the house, sometimes only 20 by 45 feet. The basement floor, which usually was partly below ground and partly above, consisted of a family dining room in front and a kitchen in back, with access to the rear yard and service alley. In cities without alleys, the service entrance usually was a door underneath a stairway leading to the front door, which was located on the right or left side of the facade.

The front door opened into a long hall with a stairway along the wall leading to the upper floors. The front room was the parlor, and the back served as another parlor or a formal dining room. The upper floors consisted of bedrooms and, after the introduction of running water in the 1840s and 1850s, a bathroom at the back of the hallway overlooking the rear yard, which previously was the site of the rain water cistern and the privy.

In crowded eastern cities, the row house remained the favorite dwelling until the late 19th century and sometimes beyond. After the Civil War, however, builders in cities such as Chicago and San Francisco erected groups of single-family dwellings that looked like traditional row houses except that they were separated from one another on the sides, often by no more than four or five feet, thereby enabling the residents to feel that they lived in a freestanding house. The detached row houses were also popular because their facades lent themselves to the greater variety of architectural expression favored by the post–Civil War styles such as Queen Anne and Richardsonian Romanesque.

With the arrival of reliable commuter trains, trolleys and cable cars in the late 19th century and the automobile in the early 20th, once-remote outlying land was brought within an easy journey of city jobs, shopping and schools. The row house ceased to be the favored dwelling of the middle and upper middle class as more and more Americans opted for the genuinely freestanding houses and spacious yards in what became known as the suburbs. Nevertheless, row houses are still being built in urban and suburban areas because of the same limited use of land and economies of scale in construction that made these dwellings popular several centuries ago. ★

Elfreth's Alley (1703), Philadelphia, a six-foot-wide alley lined with simple artisans' houses typical of colonial Philadelphia. (L. B. MacLeod, HABS)

Brownstones (1892–93, John C. Burne), Hamilton Heights, New York City, Romanesque Revival houses typical of the area. (New York State Office of Parks, Recreation and Historic Preservation)

Detached Italianate frame row house (1890s), San Francisco. (Joshua Freiwald)

SCHOOLHOUSES
Fred E. H. Schroeder

The characteristic form of schoolhouses was established in 1832 with the publication of a brief treatise on school architecture by William A. Alcott. Stressing the importance of fresh air, space and light, he prescribed large windows, a classroom providing separate desks for each pupil and open surroundings for recreation. For the next 130 years the basic classroom size of about 25 by 35 feet, expansive windows, high ceilings and an open setting, usually with adjacent playgrounds or athletic fields, distinguished both one-room country schools and large urban schools from other buildings.

The earliest schoolhouses in any district rarely survive: They were temporary structures of logs, planks, sod or other indigenous materials, generally resembling neighboring farm outbuildings. As the pioneer community became more settled and populous, the succeeding schoolhouses were more substantial, of frame, stone or brick, and were usually constructed by local carpenters or masons. These vernacular designs often resembled other rural communal buildings such as meetinghouses, small churches and town halls, frequently sharing the traditional bell tower and separate entrances for males and females. In many districts this was the final school form until post–World War II consolidation and standardization.

From the 19th century on, education reformers advocated improved school buildings. Practical interior reforms related to illumination, sanitation, ventilation, furniture, equipment and, in urban schools, special-purpose rooms. Improved exterior designs were justified on the basis that good architecture was supposed to contribute a moral influence on the formation of character. Exteriors tended to mirror current stylistic tastes. By 1860 plan books had become common, with Greek and Gothic Revival designs dominating. Rural

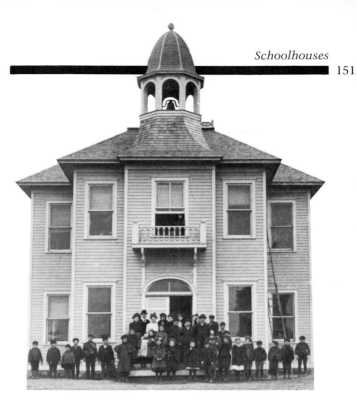

Two-story clapboard school (c. 1890), Barnes County, N.D., an unusually large and stylistically sophisticated rural school. (State Historical Society of North Dakota)

A little red schoolhouse (1813), Prescott, Mass., an example of the type that inspired the pervasive myth. (HABS)

Opposite: East Lansing School (c. 1900), near Groton, N.Y., 1907. The flag raising signaled the start of the school day. (Verne Morton, DeWitt Historical Society)

Log school (c. 1880), near Rushville, Neb., typical of the first schools built by settlers in a new community. (Nebraska State Historical Society)

Cobblestone school (1819), District No. 5, Childs, N.Y., a material indigenous to this area but rare elsewhere. The Greek Revival school has a bell tower and double entrances common on country schools. (Jack E. Boucher, HABS)

School, Baker County, Ore., 1939, an archetypal schoolroom furnished with portraits of Washington and Lincoln and a potbellied stove. (Dorothea Lange, FSA)

Old Central High School (1891–92, Emmet S. Palmer and Lucien P. Hall), Duluth, a massive Richardsonian Romanesque urban school. (St. Louis County Historical Society)

Wyoming Valley Schoolhouse (1957, Frank Lloyd Wright), Wyoming Valley, Wis., one of the few architect-designed country schools. (© Frank Lloyd Wright Foundation)

Greenbelt Center Elementary School (1936, Ellington and Wadsworth), Greenbelt, Md., an Art Deco school. (Marjory Collins, FSA)

builders copied the one-room designs, often simplifying details, while cities engaged architects to execute designs that appealed to the community. Many states began to issue plan books after the 1890s, and in the 1930s federal WPA designs dotted the rural landscapes. Individual architect-designed rural elementary schools are extremely rare; Frank Lloyd Wright's 1957 Wyoming Valley, Wis., two-room school is one of these exceptions.

The American tradition of local district control dictated that urban schools were usually designed by regional firms or city staff architects. From the 1880s to the depression, urban schools were often monumental in scale with exquisite detailing, particularly in Richardsonian Romanesque, Queen Anne, Beaux-Arts and neoclassical styles. Parochial school design history is similar, although the style of the parish church often influenced materials and ornamentation. Private boarding academies, most common in the northeastern states, are more closely related to college architecture. After World War II, the International Style of "learning factories" burgeoned along with the Baby Boom, suburban housing developments and school busing, but the basic classroom, large windows and open setting remained unchanged until the late 1960s, when open space schools eliminated walls, corridors and windows. A decade later, declining enrollments forced the closing or recycling of many city schools.

Only about 830 of the 200,000 country schools in existence around 1900 remain in use, but rural schoolhouses have been preserved and reused as houses, museums, shops and community centers. Urban school buildings have found new uses as school administrative offices and storage space, social service agency offices, shopping centers, retirement apartments and condominiums. ★

SKYSCRAPERS
Ada Louise Huxtable

The skyscraper and the 20th century are synonymous; the tall building is the landmark of our age. As a structural marvel that breaks the traditional limits on mankind's persistent ambition to build to the heavens, the skyscraper is this century's most stunning architectural phenomenon. From the Tower of Babel onward, the fantasies of builders have been vertical rather than horizontal.

In its most familiar and exhilarating aspect, the skyscraper has been a celebration of modern building technology. But it is just as much a product of zoning and tax law, the real estate and money markets, code and client requirements, energy and aesthetics, politics and speculation. Not least is the fact that it is the biggest investment game in town.

The skyscraper has totally changed the scale and appearance and concept of cities and the perceptions of people in them; it is Orwellian or Olympian, depending on how you look at it. For the skyscraper is not only the building of the century, it is also the single work of architecture that can be studied as the embodiment and expression of much that makes the century what it is. The tall building probes our collective psyche as it probes the sky.

Looking at the whole historical spectrum of skyscraper design, we can identify four significant phases: the functional, the eclectic, the modern and the postmodern. It is significant that all of the most important structural solutions came early in the development of the tall building, in a remarkably short space of time. Because these structures were concentrated in Chicago in the two decades at the end of the last century, other burgeoning cities quickly acknowledged the "Chicago style" in their commercial construction. A unique combination of industrialization, business and real estate came together in Chicago and New York for the development of a new and distinctive building type: the American office building.

In this first, or functional, phase of a new structural phenomenon, architecture was the servant of engineering. Rapid increases in building height were made possible by advances in fireproofing, metal framing and the passenger elevator, as well as by less glamorous improvements in footings and foundations, plumbing, heating, lighting and ventilation. Much larger buildings were encouraged by the rapid erection of the metal frame and curtain wall, the growth of cities and business, and the need and desire to house commercial operations that employed many people on increasingly congested and expensive urban sites. The priorities of the men who put up these buildings were economy, efficiency, size and speed. The early structures were as handsome as they were utilitarian.

The second phase of skyscraper design sought solutions through academic sources and historical precedents. This eclectic phase, which was fueled by the ascendance of the Academy and the popularity of the Beaux-Arts in this country, continued well into the 20th century, until both debate and construction were stopped by the depression. The eclectic phase produced some of the skyscraper's most remarkable monuments.

Home Insurance Building (1885, William Le Baron Jenney), Chicago, one of the earliest office skyscrapers. (Chicago Historical Society)

Prudential (Guaranty) Building (1894–95, Adler and Sullivan), Buffalo, with elaborate, typically Sullivanesque detailing. (Jack E. Boucher, HABS)

Schiller Building (1892, Adler and Sullivan), Chicago, illustrating early tripartite design principles—base, shaft and elaborate crowning cornice. (Janis Erims, HABS)

Chrysler Building (1928–30, William Van Alen), New York City, a 77-story Art Deco skyscraper with the upper floors forming a distinctive cap. (© 1980 Cervin Robinson)

Johnson Wax Administration Building and Research Tower (1936–39, Frank Lloyd Wright), Racine, Wis., a noted example of Wright's commercial design reflecting his emphasis on rounded organic forms.

The early modern, or International Style, skyscrapers are few in number; they required clients with cash, courage and a highly developed sense of aesthetic mission. Theoretically, the combination of form and function these buildings endorsed was supposed to be beyond style; actually, style was their most enduring product. By mid-century, modernism and the skyscraper were synonymous. The modern style has produced a superb skyscraper vernacular, probably the handsomest and most useful set of architectural conventions since the Georgian row house. This vernacular accommodates inhuman size, mass and bulk with an appropriate and saving simplicity.

The fourth, or current, phase of skyscraper design, called postmodern, is exploring many new avenues of design. The most conspicuous and questionable characteristic of this development is the renunciation and devaluation of everything the modernists believed in and built. Its most encouraging aspects are the rediscovery of history and the continuum and context of the city, and the recognition of the values of diversity.

Whatever their claims to style, today's large commercial structures, like those that came before them, are essentially an economic formula. But there are other, less pragmatic factors that influence the decision to build tall. The desire to convey image, status, power and prestige, to signal economic or cultural dominance, is universally acknowledged. There is, finally, in the words of the Council on Tall Buildings, the basic human desire "to build to the very limits of strength and knowledge . . . to achieve the limits of the achievable." This is the ultimate, eternal and irresistible challenge. ★

Rockefeller Center (1931–40, Raymond Hood), New York City, a skyscraper city within a city. The 70-story RCA Building stands in the center of the development. (Courtesy Rockefeller Center, Inc.)

House of Seagram (1957, Ludwig Mies van der Rohe and Philip Johnson), New York City, the International Style precursor of contemporary "glass box" skyscrapers. (Philip Johnson Collection)

AT&T Corporate Headquarters (1983, John Burgee Architects with Philip Johnson), New York City, with its "Chippendale" cornice. (© Richard Payne AIA 1984)

Portland Building (1982, Michael Graves), Portland, Ore., a postmodern skyscraper with historical allusions. (Proto Acme)

SUBURBS
Gwendolyn Wright

Suburbs imply a close relationship to a city, counterbalanced by rural characteristics of spaciousness, greenery and village togetherness, all self-consciously preserved—or sometimes created. Suburbs also embody, and thereby strengthen, certain American cultural norms: the desire for homogeneous communities and individualistic display, a sentimental feeling for tradition and a fascination with modern technology.

By the early 1800s villages such as Cambridge, outside Boston, and Brooklyn, across the river from New York, had become primarily residential suburbs for commuters. The first professionally planned suburbs came at mid-century with Andrew Jackson Davis's Llewelyn Park, N.J. (1853), and Frederick Law Olmsted's Riverside (1869), near Chicago. Romantic planning combined into a new suburban package the designers' sensitivity to topography and the developers' recognition of desires for health, recreation and nature.

The first great migration to the suburbs came with improved public transportation after the Civil War. Most speculative subdivisions followed a regular gridiron street system, broken by occasional diagonal avenues and small parks. Although lots and house plans were basically identical, builders suggested the particularity of each dwelling with ornamented facades. Other suburbs united work and residence in company towns. Pullman (1884), south of Chicago, is the most famous example of how an industrialist could attract skilled workers and maintain paternalistic control in a planned suburb.

Suburbs of the early 1900s promoted regionalism with local materials and local history—or historical myth. Stucco Spanish colonial motifs found favor in California and antebellum Greek Revival porticoes in the South, while colonial and Tudor houses appeared everywhere. A modern regional prototype, the Prairie Style, evolved in midwestern suburbs such as Oak Park, Ill. Elsewhere, traditional ties were loosened, however, as the compact bungalow and the automobile encouraged many working-class families to leave inner-city ethnic neighborhoods for industrial suburbs such as River Rouge, Mich.

Wealthier suburbs increasingly exerted controls over design, land use and residents themselves. This first occurred in thematic areas for small shops, such as Station Square (1912) at Forest Hills Gardens in Queens, N.Y., by Grosvenor Atterbury. (These anticipated the suburban shopping centers of the 1920s, which added parking lots.) Entire new communities had architectural review boards; the Country Club District, in Kansas City, Mo., won international renown for its controls. In many suburbs, zoning relegated businesses, industry and multi-family dwellings to a "strip" beyond the gates and walls that defined the suburb's boundaries, while restrictive covenants prohibited minorities. Several model suburbs sought to promote bucolic communities through modern planning techniques. Stein and Wright's Radburn, N.J. (1929), and the Greenbelt towns of the New Deal became famous total visions of suburban life—organized around family, community and the car.

The federal government indirectly but massively

Oak Park, Ill. (1860s), a bird's-eye view drawn by Augustus Koch. This suburb later became famous for its Prairie Style buildings. (Historical Society of Oak Park and River Forest)

Riverside, Ill. (1869, Olmsted, Vaux and Company). The landscaping scheme incorporating parks and woodlands was a trademark of Frederick Law Olmsted.

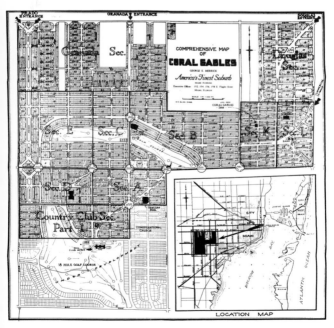

Coral Gables, Fla. (1920s), envisioned and planned by builder George E. Merrick as a city of Spanish-style buildings. (G. E. Merrick Collection, Historical Museum of Southeast Florida and the Caribbean)

Greenbelt, Md. (1936), a federally sponsored planned suburb that was part of Franklin D. Roosevelt's New Deal. Most of the housing is Art Deco in style. (Marjory Collins, FSA)

Radburn, N.J. (1929, Clarence Stein and Henry Wright), a community incorporating cul-de-sacs, a central commons and separate pedestrian and automobile traffic. (Newark Public Library)

sponsored suburban development after World War II with FHA-financed home mortgages, tax credits for mortgages and federal highways. Levittown (1947), Long Island, N.Y. was the epitome of mass-produced, moderate-cost suburbia. Other developers soon picked up the built-in features, open house plans, carports and cul-de-sac streets. In California the ranch house emerged as builder Joseph Eichler hired local architectural firms to design model houses with picture windows and patios for thousands of subdivisions.

Master-planned new towns of the 1960s and 1970s, such as Reston, Va. (1964), and Columbia, Md. (1967), tried to provide alternatives to acknowledged suburban problems. At a smaller level, the Planned Unit Development (PUD) grouped houses and townhouses in clusters to conserve open land as shared public spaces.

Today, while the suburbs remain the dominant American residential prototype, they still reveal a deep cultural ambivalence about social and formal diversity. Present efforts to rezone existing suburbs and provide more variety in new ones show the continuing efforts to combine the best of both country and city life. ★

Levittown, N.Y. (1947), which became synonymous with the auto-mobile-oriented, middle-class suburbs of the 1950s. (Levittown Public Library)

Lake Anne, Reston, Va. (1964), one of the few planned new towns that succeeded and has continued to grow. (Reston Land Corporation)

Detail of some of the original townhouses on Reston's Lake Anne. (Reston Land Corporation)

THEATERS AND MOVIE HOUSES
Craig Morrison

Although slow to develop, the theater became a building type whose grandeur and technical refinement were unparalleled in American architecture.

The puritanical social environment of colonial America frowned on the drama, so performances were often held in ballrooms and other nontheatrical meeting halls. Except for notable examples in major cities, theaters were spartan, a pattern that persisted for a century in small towns, where plays generally were presented in a hall above a store that was rudimentary in equipment, simply decorated and uncomfortable.

In the 1850s the form of the Continental opera house was borrowed for the American theater. Within a relatively simple exterior was contained a rich auditorium characterized by a high, square proscenium arch, two or more narrow horseshoe-shaped balconies supported by numerous slim columns, lavishly decorated box seats overlooking the stage, a painted drop curtain, a profusion of allegorical paintings and sculptures and, usually, a great central chandelier. The finest of these mid-century theaters, the Academy of Music (1855–56, LeBrun and Runge), Philadelphia, remains the unquestioned queen of America's historic theater buildings.

Although usually seen as a decorator's architecture, the theater actually presented a difficult amalgam of technological needs—sight lines, acoustics, fire safety, lighting, ventilation and sufficient standardization to permit travelling shows to fit their properties into one theater after another. During the latter part of the 19th century, several architects perfected these requirements and devel-

Walnut Street Theatre (1809; 1820s, John Haviland), Philadelphia, the oldest theater in continuous use in the English-speaking world. (C. Burton)

Academy of Music (1855–56, LeBrun and Runge), Philadelphia, the oldest music auditorium in continuous use in this country. (NTHP Collection)

oped practices devoted exclusively to theater design. The demand for entertainment in the rapidly expanding central and western states created a nationwide need for their services. The most active designer was J. B. McElfatrick of New York, who designed more than 200 theaters in locations as diverse as Atlanta, Seattle, Detroit and San Antonio. To the credit of these men, virtually every city in the West had a Grand Opera House equipped to mount elaborate productions. The theaters were elegantly appointed, elaborate and often exotic in style.

The moving picture was first presented in converted stores, but the rapid growth of its popularity prompted a new wave of theater construction. To allow better viewing of the flat screen, the new theater had a single deep balcony in which all seats faced forward, rather than the old horseshoe galleries. The intimacy associated with the live stage was replaced by size and grandeur. Theaters doubled in capacity, appointments became ever more rich, and special effects were introduced such as colored cove lighting, mighty pipe organs, goldfish swimming in marble fountains and even floating clouds projected on blue sky-dome ceilings dotted with twinkling electric stars. The description of one palace as "an acre of seats in a garden of dreams" reflected the architect's goal to bring an oasis of regal elegance into the lives of a newly urbanized industrial populace, whose work and living environments often were tedious and plain.

In recent years, suburbanization and in-home entertainment have sapped the nightly congregations that gathered in great downtown theaters, and many of these fine buildings have been lost. An increasing number, though, are being restored and function well as performing arts centers, helping to ensure the endurance of their beauty. ★

Right and below: Paradise Theatre (1928, John Eberson), Chicago, one of the most opulent
movie theaters of this period.
(Theater Historical Society of
America Archives; Clarkson N.
Potter)

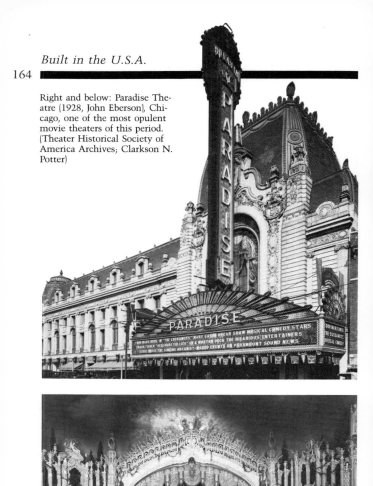

Fox Theatre (1929, Olivier Vinour),
Atlanta, with a Moorish Revival
interior. (Floyd Jillson, Atlanta Jour-
nal-Constitution Magazine)

Paramount Arts Centre (1931, Rapp
and Rapp), Aurora, Ill., with Art
Deco interior decoration. (Paramount Arts Centre)

Mount Vernon Theatre (1910, A. B. Mullett and Company), Washington, D.C., a nickelodeon with an entrance arch. (Craig Morrison and Janet Hochuli, HABS)

Left and below: Ryman Auditorium (Grand Ole Opry House) (1889–92, A. T. Thompson), Nashville, built as a revival tabernacle and later famous for country music performances. (Jack E. Boucher, HABS)

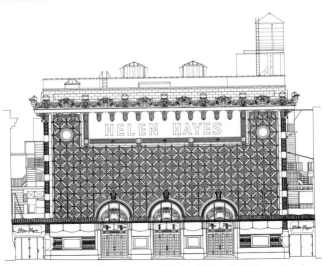

Helen Hayes Theater (1911, Herts and Tallant), New York City, a Broadway landmark lost to redevelopment. (Robert Hartman, Meadows/Woll Architects, HABS)

Frame cabin, Berkeley County, S.C.
Until the early 20th century, many
buildings in the South were made
with such roughly finished materials. (Albert Simons, HABS)

Hancock House (1734), Hancock
Bridge, N.J., with brick patterning
characteristic of the mid-Atlantic
colonies. (E. Ray Coutch, HABS)

Morehead-Gano Log House
(c. 1850), near Grapevine, Tex., a
dog-trot structure. The central
breezeway is a regional response to
climate. (Anthony Crosby, HABS)

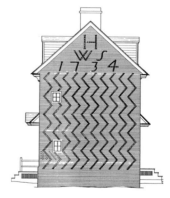

Jordan-Pierson House (c. 1795), near
Davisboro, Ga., a modified dog-trot
plan with the breezeway reduced to
a small central hall. (Kenneth Kay)

VERNACULAR BUILDINGS
Dell Upton

Vernacular building is ordinary building. It is not a type in the sense of a single easily recognizable form with a specific function and a limited number of formal characteristics, as a barn is a type. Neither is it a style, like the Federal style or the Second Empire style, in the sense of a characteristic visual expression linking buildings of disparate types. Instead, vernacular architecture includes buildings of many types and functions, buildings with decoration drawn from all styles and from no particular style. Vernacular buildings can be thought of as the visual embodiment of a social process, in which available architectural ideas from many sources, local and international, traditional and novel, are shaped into buildings answering the special requirements of a social class, an economic group or a local or ethnic community.

To define vernacular building by the process that creates it rather than by the product means that it is more difficult (and probably not necessary) to pigeonhole individual buildings. It is relatively easy, however, to suggest some of the kinds or groups of buildings in which the vernacular process can be observed most readily. Foremost among these are houses, for living spaces are closely attuned to the changing forms of that most elementary institution of most human societies, the family. House plans embody economic restraints and productive activities, patterns of work and play and the structures of gender and generational interaction. Both the social forms and the architectural containers vary from time to time, place to place and class to class, yet from the 17th-century framed house to the 20th-century apartment block, students of vernacular architecture have found the house the most fascinating of American vernacular buildings.

Structures characteristic of certain occupational groups can also be thought of as vernacular buildings. Three examples will illustrate. Agricultural buildings are the most obviously "vernacular." They must be suited to the crops, agricultural practices and climatic characteristics of their localities. The size, shape and internal arrangements of industrial buildings such as textile mills are closely controlled by power sources, light requirements and the spatial demands of the machinery employed, as well as the social organization of industrial labor. At the same time the particular visual appearance of a given mill might also be affected by the owner's interest in appearing architecturally up to date and, even more important, by a desire to be inconspicuous or assertive, according to the degree of community acceptance of the presence of the mill.

Since the 18th century, small stores have incorporated a large, shelf-lined room, with customers' and merchants' territories separated by waist-high counters set parallel to the walls. Beside or behind this display room is a small counting room. This characteristic form is evidence of a remarkable stability in the social relations and spatial organization of small-scale commerce.

To these traditional examples of occupational vernacular architecture can be added modern structures such as roadside commercial buildings that serve not rural communities, the working class or farming populations

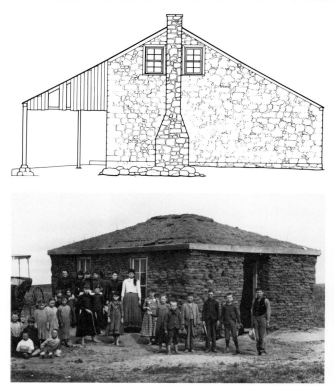

Sod school with hipped roof, Custer County, Neb., 1891. This county, which covered 2,552 square miles, in 1910 had 8,000 sod houses and probably dozens of sod schoolhouses. (Solomon D. Butcher Collection, Nebraska State Historical Society)

but large numbers of middle-class, automobile-dependent Americans and that vary little from place to place.

Vernacular building is often described as un-self-conscious or purely utilitarian architecture. In fact, vernacular buildings are the products of conscious choices by their builders. Vernacular designers use local stone and wood, but they also use steel, glass and plastic. They draw on traditional decoration and plans, but they also incorporate classical, Gothic and hybrid decorations as well as unique and currently popular plan elements in their designs. The key to understanding vernacular building is the notion of process. Fashion and aesthetic ideas are incorporated into vernacular building, but they are subordinated to the more immediate purposes of the farmer, the storekeeper, the householder, the speculative builder and the fast-food merchant. It is this quality of complex response to indigenous demands, rather than to abstract intellectual or aesthetic concepts, that makes vernacular building ordinary building: It is architecture in the service of large groups of people, and consequently it dominates the landscape.

Vernacular architecture is chameleonlike; it can change as rapidly as its context does. Some forms survive for decades, even centuries, but others vanish within a few years. Cherished folk forms like log houses and large wooden barns are rarely built any longer, and their numbers are diminishing, but this does not mean the end of vernacular building. As long as people build, there will be vernacular architecture. ★

Opposite: Aue Stagecoach Inn (c. 1855), Leon Springs, Tex., a stone structure with a simple porte cochere. (Larry Hermsen, HABS)

Shotgun houses (1850s), Louisville, Ky., which had a hall extending the length of the house along one side and which were only one room wide. (Preservation Alliance, Louisville, Ky.)

Workers' houses (c. 1900), Mobile, Ala., examples of shotgun houses. (Jack E. Boucher, HABS)

House (c. 1860), near De Armanville, Ala., an extended I house with sheds. (Bob Gamble)

General store and post office (late 19th century), Philomont, Va. (Wm. Edmund Barrett)

Interior, general store, Colvin Run Mill, Fairfax, Va. (Fairfax County Park Authority)

Tobacco barn, Brown County, Ind., a vernacular farm building used as a sign. (Balthazar Korab)

Corn crib, De Clerque Farm, Closter, N.J. (C. P. Johnson, HABS)

Feed store, Tomball, Tex., 1945, clearly announcing one of its main products. (Esther Bubley, Standard Oil of New Jersey Collection)

ZOOS
R. L. Blakely

The architecture of zoos has been influenced more by what people have felt about animals than by the dominant architectural standards of the day. Zoos are ancient institutions; 4,000 years ago they already had a venerable history. The first known zoos in China, Egypt and the Middle East were large parks that featured both exotic plants and tame animals that roamed freely. These parks, owned by royalty and wealthy individuals, were not open to the public. In China one such park was called the "Garden of Knowledge." Around the Mediterranean such parks were known by the Greek word "paradeisos," which later Hebrew scholars modified to the word "paradise."

The oldest zoos in the United States were built only a little more than a century ago. Some of these zoos, such as those in Cincinnati, Philadelphia and Chicago's Lincoln Park, continue to thrive. As new developments in zoo culture arose, existing buildings were remodeled or replaced so that these institutions are quite modern. Little effort has been made to retain the old structures as interesting relics of the past.

Early in this century, during what might be called the scientific age, many U.S. cities added zoos to their list of cultural institutions. Science and technology were making rapid strides and were powerful shapers of our earlier zoos. Taxonomy, the scientific classification of plants and animals, required that animals be displayed together in closely related groups. Monkeys, birds, reptiles and felines, for example, were each displayed in their own sections of the zoo in order to show the wonderful variety of nature. The rather new concepts about germs and sanitation dictated that cages be of concrete, tile and steel—easy to keep sanitary. And what of the animals themselves, relegated to row upon row of sanitary cages arranged by the dictates of taxonomy? Ivan Pavlov, the Russian psychologist, had just demonstrated the conditioned reflex. To many animal psychologists, his experiments showed that animals were little more than living robots, motivated only by a mysterious force called instinct.

Two developments in the 1920s were to have a decided effect on zoos everywhere. One was the creation, in

New York Zoological Park (c. 1870), Bronx, N.Y., with sculptor A. P. Proctor working on decorations for the elephant house. (© New York Zoological Society)

Elephant area, National Zoological Park, Washington, D.C., showing naturalistic-style enclosures. (Carleton Knight III)

Opposite: Lincoln Park Zoo (c. 1870), Chicago, c. 1900. (Chicago Historical Society)

Germany, of a zoo that used moats, rather than fences and bars, to restrain animals. The father of this new concept was Carl Hagenback, whose naturalistic approach allowed visitors to imagine how Africa or Asia might really look.

The other influencing factor was the depression and its offspring, the Works Progress Administration. Cities found their zoo attendance swelling with millions of visitors who could afford few other forms of entertainment. They also found that the federal government was willing, even eager, to undertake such projects as building new zoos and adding to existing ones.

In taking advantage of the federal largess, some zoos chose to stay with tradition. Massive buildings of classical design were erected in stone and concrete. Their grand scale, with imposing colonaded facades, made a zoo's lion house look hardly different from the local art museum or public library. Others opted to follow Hagenback's concept. St. Louis, Detroit and Chicago's Brookfield zoos are excellent examples of this naturalistic approach, which remains popular to this day.

Zoos that have been built within the last two decades have reflected a more enlightened and more generous attitude toward animals. The truly fascinating aspects of animals are not their differences from us but rather their similarities to us—the common threads that weave together the community of life. Plants as well as animals are emphasized as partners in the business of life. Large mixed groups of creatures are shown in habitats resembling their fast-disappearing wild homes. Efforts are made to show what the animal is and does rather than what abstract scientific principle it may illustrate. These newest zoos, such as those in Louisville, Ky., Columbia, S.C., and Wichita, Kans., seem almost to have returned to the plan of the very first zoos—those that were called "paradise." ★

Opposite: Bear pits (1874, Theophilus Parsons Chandler, Jr.), Philadelphia Zoological Gardens, the first zoo in the country. (Cortlandt V. D. Hubbard, HABS)

Anteater in front of the Small Mammal House (1935, Edwin H. Clark), National Zoological Park, Washington, D.C. (Jessie Cohen, National Zoological Park)

Reptile House (1929, Albert L. Harris), with a modern addition, National Zoological Park, Washington, D.C. (Jessie Cohen, National Zoological Park)

Wisner Children's Village (1930s), Audubon Zoological Gardens, New Orleans, built by the WPA and modeled after a Louisiana plantation pigeonnier. (William Lake Douglas, Design Consortium, Ltd.)

Entrance pavilions (1874, Furness and Hewitt), Philadelphia Zoological Gardens, Philadelphia, a Victorian Gothic structure. (Jack E. Boucher, HABS)

Contributors

R. L. Blakely is director of the Sedgwick County Zoo, Wichita, Kans., and past president of the American Association of Zoological Parks and Aquariums. He began his zoo career at age 15, was general curator of Lincoln Park Zoo in Chicago and was later director of Chicago's Brookfield Zoo.

George S. Bobinski is dean and professor at the School of Information and Library Studies, State University of New York, Buffalo. He is author of *Carnegie Libraries* and has helped plan both academic and public library buildings.

Padraic Burke is a historic preservation consultant as well as a developer of historic property in Seattle and Spokane. His interest in the revival of public markets has produced several articles, including "To Market, To Market."

S. Allen Chambers, Jr., is an architectural historian with the Historic American Buildings Survey, National Park Service, Washington, D.C. He is author of *Lynchburg: An Architectural History* and coauthor of *What Style Is It? A Guide to American Architecture.* His first piggy bank was a model of a typical classical bank.

Alvin G. Davis is executive vice president and general manager of the Ranching Heritage Association, Inc., and the Endowment for the Preservation of Ranching Heritage of America, Inc., Lubbock, Tex.

Bob Easton is an architect in Santa Barbara, Calif., and coauthor of the forthcoming *Native American Architecture.* He is also coauthor and designer of *Domebooks, Shelter* and *Santa Barbara Architecture.*

Everett L. Fly, a landscape architect, and **La Barbara Wigfall Fly,** a planner and urban designer, are the founders of Entourage, Inc., in San Antonio, Tex., a research and education organization. Recent projects have focused on the preservation of black communities and include a planning and design study of black settlements in America.

Frederick Fried, a writer, lecturer and museum consultant, and **Mary Fried,** an artist, are coauthors of *America's Forgotten Folk Arts* and live in New York City. Frederick Fried also is author of *A Pictorial History of the Carousel, Fragmentary Landmarks, Artists in Wood* and *New York Civic Sculpture.*

David Gebhard is professor of architectural history, University of California, Santa Barbara, and curator of the architectural drawing collection in the University Art Museum. He is a contributor to *California Crazy: Roadside Vernacular Architecture* and coauthor of *Architecture in Los Angeles: A Complete Guide, A Guide to Architecture in San Francisco and Northern California* and *Two Hundred Years of American Architectural Drawings.*

Paul Goeldner, AIA, is author of "Architectural History of the American Courthouse" in *A Courthouse Conservation Handbook.* He visited more than 500 courthouses in 1968–69 in preparation for his Columbia University doctoral dissertation, "Temples of Justice: Nineteenth-Century County Courthouses in the Midwest and Texas." An architect with the National Park Service in Washington, D.C., he also is author of the *Utah Catalog: Historic American Buildings Survey.*

Martin Greif is vice president and editorial director of the Main Street Press, Pittstown, N.J. He is author of *The Airport Book, Depression Modern: The Thirties Style in America, The New Industrial Landscape* and other books on architecture and decorative arts.

Richard J. S. Gutman is author of *American Diner* and architect for restorations of a lunch wagon and diner at the Henry Ford Museum and Greenfield Village. He also has lectured across the country on diners. He lives in West Roxbury, Mass.

John Hancock is professor of urban planning at the University of Washington, Seattle, and author of "The Apartment House in Urban America" in *Buildings and Society.* His research and published works focus on the history and societal context of American housing, planning and city development.

John Fraser Hart is professor of geography at the University of Minnesota, Minneapolis. His research has focused on the ways in which culture, economy and environment have interacted to produce distinctive rural landscapes, especially in the United States. He is author of *The Look of the Land, The South* and *U.S. and Canada* and editor of *Regions of the United States.*

Herbert H. Harwood, Jr., is a professional railroader and amateur railroad historian. He is an official of the Chessie System Railroads, Baltimore, Md., author of several books on railroad history and a spare-time industrial archeologist and documentary photographer.

F. Ross Holland, Jr., is author of *America's Lighthouses* and other books and articles dealing with lighthouses. He is director of restoration and preservation for the Statue of Liberty–Ellis Island Foundation, Inc., New York City.

Thomas C. Hubka is author of *Big House, Little House, Back House, Barn: The Connected Farm Buildings of New England* and associate professor in the Department of Architecture, University of Oregon, Eugene.

Ada Louise Huxtable is the former architecture critic of the *New York Times* and is author of *The Tall Building Artistically Reconsidered: The Search for a Skyscraper Style, Will They Ever Finish Bruckner Boulevard?, Kicked a Building Lately?* and *Goodbye History, Hello Hamburger.* She received the Pulitzer Prize in 1970 for her architectural criticism and has been honored also by the American Institute of Architects and the National Trust.

Steven Izenour is senior associate in the architectural firm of Venturi, Rauch and Scott Brown, Philadelphia, and design critic at the School of Architecture, University of Pennsylvania. He is coauthor of *Learning from Las Vegas* and *White Towers* and has spent more than 15 years documenting the architecture of the American roadside.

Donald C. Jackson is a historical engineering consultant and author of *Great American Bridges and Dams.* Formerly an engineering historian with the Historic American Engineering Record, National Park Service, Washington, D.C., he has taught at the University of Pennsylvania, Philadelphia.

William L. Lebovich is author of *America's City Halls* and has contributed a chapter on Eero Saarinen for *The AIA Gold Medal.* He is an architectural historian with the Historic American Buildings Survey, National Park Service, Washington, D.C.

Jeffrey W. Limerick is coauthor of *America's Grand Resort Hotels* and an architect in Boulder, Colo. He taught architectural theory, history and design at Yale University from 1974 to 1980.

Charles Lockwood is author of six books, including *Bricks and Brownstone, The Guide to Hollywood and Beverly Hills* and *Dream Palaces: Hollywood at Home,* as well as numerous articles, and coauthor of *The Estates of Beverly Hills.* He lives in Los Angeles.

Richard Longstreth is associate professor of architectural history and director of the graduate historic preservation program, George Washington University, Washington, D.C. He has prepared a typology of Main Street buildings for *The Buildings of Main Street*. Author of *On the Edge of the World: Four Architects in San Francisco at the Turn of the Century*, he is chairman of the Society of Architectural Historians' Preservation committee and is on the board of Preservation Action.

Robert B. MacKay is director of the Society for the Preservation of Long Island Antiquities, Setauket, N.Y. He wrote his 1980 doctoral dissertation at Boston University on aspects of American prison design in the 19th century.

Charles W. Moore is an architect and principal of Urban Innovations Group, Los Angeles. He is coauthor of several books, including *The Place of Houses* and *Home, Sweet Home* and has designed many houses, including the award-winning condominiums at Sea Ranch, Calif. He has taught at the Yale University School of Architecture and currently is a professor at the University of Texas.

Craig Morrison is manager of restoration services, Studio Four, Vitetta Group, Philadelphia. For several years as an architect with the Historic American Buildings Survey, National Park Service, he directed an American theater recording project.

Dianne Newell is a Canadian historian specializing in 19th-century industrial processes and architecture and is author of "With Respect to Breweries." A former president of the Society for Industrial Archeology, she currently teaches at the University of British Columbia, Vancouver, B.C.

Donald E. Pitzer is executive director of the National Historic Communal Societies Association and director of the Center for Communal Studies, Indiana State University, Evansville, where he is chairman of the history department. He has lectured and written widely on communal societies and serves on the editorial board of the journal *Communal Societies*.

Willard B. Robinson is professor of architecture at Texas Tech University, Lubbock. He has served as consultant for the restoration and interpretation of several forts, including Fort Adams, R.I., and Fort Loudoun, Tenn., and is author of *American Forts*.

Thomas J. Schlereth is professor of American studies and director of the graduate American studies program, University of Notre Dame, Notre Dame, Ind. He is author of *The University of Notre Dame: A Portrait of Its History and Campus* and *U.S. 40: A Roadscape of the American Experience*, as well as books on material culture research.

Fred E. H. Schroeder is author of several articles on schoolhouses, including "Educational Legacy: Rural One-Room Schoolhouses" and "The Little Red Schoolhouse." He began his teaching career in a one-room school in Wisconsin and is currently professor of humanities at the University of Minnesota, Duluth. He is a frequent consultant to historical societies and museums.

William Seale is coauthor of *Temples of Democracy: The State Capitols of the U.S.A.* A historian in Alexandria, Va., who writes and consults on historical restorations, he is also author of *The Tasteful Interlude* and *Recreating the Historic House Interior*, among other books. He has also completed a two-volume history of the White House.

William C. Shopsin, AIA, is an architect and historic preservation consultant in New York City. He is author of *Saving Large Estates*, coauthor of *The Villard Houses: Life Story of a Landmark* and a founder of the Preservation League of New York State.

Phoebe Stanton is a consultant on architectural design and previously taught art history at the Johns Hopkins University, Baltimore, Md. She is author of *The Gothic Revival in American Church Architecture* and a contributor to *The Houses of Parliament* and has written on architecture for various journals.

John D. Thompson is coauthor of *The Hospital* and author of numerous publications and articles on hospitals and health management. He is director of the hospital administration program and professor at the Yale University School of Medicine, New Haven, Conn., and holds several other professorships at Yale University.

William H. Tishler is professor of landscape architecture at the University of Wisconsin, Madison. He is author of numerous publications on landscape architecture and historic preservation, including "The Site Arrangement of Rural Farmsteads," and a contributor to *New Directions in Rural Preservation* and has received a variety of awards for his professional achievements.

Dell Upton is assistant professor of architectural history, Department of Architecture, University of California, Berkeley, and editor of the *Vernacular Architecture Newsletter.* His publications include *Holy Things and Profane: Anglican Parish Churches in Colonial Virginia* and *Common Places: Readings in Vernacular Architecture.*

Daniel I. Vieyra is author of *"Fill 'Er Up": An Architectural History of America's Gas Stations.* Formerly preservation architect for the city of Trenton, N.J., he is currently director of the graduate historic preservation program, School of Architecture, Kent State University, Kent, Ohio.

Robert M. Vogel is curator of the Division of Mechanical and Civil Engineering, National Museum of American History, Smithsonian Institution, Washington, D.C., and has extensive experience as a consultant, lecturer and author on industrial archeology. He is an officer of the Society for Industrial Archeology and other professional organizations and is chairman of the Maryland state review board for the National Register of Historic Places.

Gwendolyn Wright is author of *Moralism and the Model Home* and *Building the Dream: A Social History of Housing in America.* She received her Master of Architecture and Ph.D. degrees from the University of California, Berkeley. She now teaches urban and architectural history at Columbia University, New York City.

Rebecca Zurier received a Youthgrant from the National Endowment for the Humanities to travel across America studying the architecture of firehouses, which resulted in her book, *The American Firehouse.* She is now a doctoral candidate in art history at Yale University, New Haven, Conn.

Further Reading

General Sources

Craig, Lois. *The Federal Presence: Architecture, Politics, and Symbols in U.S. Government Building.* Cambridge, Mass.: MIT Press, 1978.

Fitch, James Marston. *American Building 1: The Historical Forces That Shaped It.* Boston: Houghton Mifflin, 1966.

King, Anthony D. *Buildings and Society: Essays on the Social Development of the Built Environment.* London and Boston: Routledge and Kegan Paul, 1980.

National Trust for Historic Preservation. "Form and Function," *All About Old Buildings: The Whole Preservation Catalog.* Washington, D.C.: Preservation Press, 1985.

Pevsner, Nikolaus. *A History of Building Types.* Princeton, N.J.: Princeton University Press, 1976.

Rifkind, Carole. *A Field Guide to American Architecture.* New York: New American Library, 1980.

Whiffen, Marcus, and Frederick Koeper. *American Architecture, 1607–1976.* Cambridge, Mass.: MIT Press, 1981.

Airports

Greif, Martin. *The Airport Book: From Landing Field to Modern Terminal.* Main Street Press. New York: Mayflower Books, 1979.

Amusement Parks and Fairs

Braithwaite, David. *Fairground Architecture: The World of Amusement Parks, Carnivals and Fairs.* New York: Praeger, 1968.

Fried, Frederick. *A Pictorial History of the Carousel.* South Brunswick, N.J.: A. S. Barnes, 1964.

Fried, Frederick, and Mary Fried. *America's Forgotten Folk Arts.* New York: Pantheon Books, 1978.

Kyriazi, Gary. *The Great American Amusement Parks.* Secaucus, N.J.: Citadel, 1976.

Weedon, Geoff, and Richard Ward. *Fairground Art.* New York: Abbeville Press, 1982.

Apartment Buildings

Abel, Joseph, et al. *Apartment Houses.* New York: Reinhold, 1947.

Alpern, Andrew. *Apartments for the Affluent: A Historical Survey of Buildings in New York City.* New York: McGraw-Hill, 1975.

Hancock, John. "The Apartment House in Urban America." In *Buildings and Society.* Edited by Anthony King. London and Boston: Routledge and Kegan Paul, 1980.

Banks

Hopkins, Alfred. *The Fundamentals of Good Bank Building.* New York: Bankers Publishing, 1928.

Hoyt, Charles King, ed. *Buildings for Commerce and Industry.* New York: McGraw-Hill, 1978.

Mayer, Martin. "The Banking Story." *American Heritage,* April–May 1984.

Barns

Arthur, Eric, and Dudley Witney. *The Barn: A Vanishing Land-*

mark in North America. New York: A & W Publishers, 1975.

Fitchen, John. *The New World Dutch Barn: A Study of Its Characteristics, Its Structural System, and Its Probable Erectional Procedures.* Syracuse, N.Y.: Syracuse University Press, 1968.

Noble, Allen G. *Wood, Brick, and Stone: The North American Settlement Landscape.* Vol. 2, *Barns and Farm Structures.* Amherst: University of Massachusetts Press, 1984.

Sloane, Eric. *An Age of Barns.* New York: Ballantine, 1984.

Black Settlements

Crockett, Norman L. *The Black Towns.* Lawrence, Kans.: Regents Press, 1979.

Fly, Everett L. "Black Settlements in America, 1870–1920." *Harvard Graduate School of Design News,* May 1977.

McDaniel, George W. *Hearth and Home: Preserving a People's Culture.* Philadelphia: Temple University Press, 1982.

Schuyler, Robert L., ed. *Archaeological Perspectives on Ethnicity in America: Afro-American and Asian American Cultural History.* Farmingdale, N.Y.: Baywood, 1980.

Thum, Marcella. *Exploring Black America: A History and Guide.* New York: Atheneum, 1975.

Breweries

Newell, Dianne. "With Respect to Breweries." *Historic Preservation,* January–March 1975.

The Western Brewer. *One Hundred Years of Brewing: A Complete History of the Progress Made in the Art, Science, and Industry of Brewing in the World.* 1903. Reprint. New York: Arno Press, 1974.

Bridges

Comp, T. Allan, and Donald C. Jackson. *Bridge Truss Types: A Guide to Dating and Identifying.* Technical Leaflet Series, no. 95. Nashville: American Association for State and Local History, 1977.

Jackson, Donald C. *Great American Bridges and Dams.* Washington, D.C.: Preservation Press, 1988.

Leonhardt, Fritz. *Bridges.* Cambridge, Mass.: MIT Press, 1984.

Mock, Elizabeth B. *The Architecture of Bridges.* 1949. Reprint. New York: Arno Press, 1972.

Plowden, David. *Bridges: The Spans of North America.* 1974. Reprint. New York: W. W. Norton, 1984.

Capitols

Brown, Glenn. *History of the United States Capitol.* 1900, 1903. Reprint. New York: Da Capo Press, 1970.

Hitchcock, Henry-Russell, and William Seale. *Temples of Democracy: The State Capitols of the U.S.A.* New York: Harcourt, Brace, Jovanovich, 1976.

City Halls

Glaab, Charles, and A. Theodore Brown. *A History of Urban America.* New York: Macmillan, 1982.

Lebovich, William L. *America's City Halls.* Historic American Buildings Survey. Washington, D.C.: Preservation Press, 1984.

Colleges and Universities

Horowitz, Helen Lefkowitz. *Alma Mater: Design and Experience in the Women's Colleges from Their 19th-Century Beginnings to the 1930s.* New York: Alfred A. Knopf, 1984.

Llewellyn, Robert, and Douglas Day. *The Academical Village: Thomas Jefferson's University.* Charlottesville, Va.: Thomasson-Grant, 1982.

Turner, Paul Venable. *Campus: An American Planning Tradition.* Cambridge, Mass.: MIT Press, 1984.

Communal Societies

Hayden, Dolores. *Seven American Utopias: The Architecture of Communitarian Socialism,*

1790–1975. Cambridge, Mass.: MIT Press, 1976.

Hedgepeth, William, and Dennis Stock. *The Alternative: Communal Life in New America.* New York: Macmillan, 1970.

Kagan, Paul. *New World Utopias: A Photographic History of the Search for Community.* New York: Penguin Books, 1975.

Courthouses

Brink, Robert J., ed. *Courthouses of the Commonwealth.* Amherst: University of Massachusetts Press, 1984.

Johnson, Herbert Alan, and Ralph K. Andrist. *Historic Courthouses of New York State.* New York: Columbia University Press, 1977.

National Trust for Historic Preservation and National Clearinghouse for Criminal Justice Planning and Architecture. *A Courthouse Conservation Handbook.* Washington, D.C.: Preservation Press, 1976.

Pare, Richard, ed. *Court House: A Photographic Document.* Essay by Henry-Russell Hitchcock and William Seale. New York: Horizon Press, 1978.

Diners

Baeder, John. *Diners.* New York: Abrams, 1978.

Gutman, Richard J. S., and Elliott Kaufman, with David Slovic. *American Diner.* New York: Harper and Row, 1979.

Kaplan, Donald, and Alan Bellink. *Diners of the Northeast.* Photographs by John Bean. Stockbridge, Mass.: Berkshire Traveller Press, 1980.

Drive-ins

Belasco, Warren James. *Americans on the Road: From Autocamp to Motel, 1910–1945.* Cambridge, Mass.: MIT Press, 1979.

Gebhard, David, and Harriet Von Breton. *L.A. in the Thirties.* Salt Lake City: Peregrine Smith Books, 1975.

Heimann, Jim, and Rip George. *California Crazy: Roadside Vernacular Architecture.* Introduction by David Gebhard. San Francisco: Chronicle Books, 1980.

Margolies, John. *The End of the Road: Vanishing Highway Architecture in America.* New York: Penguin Books, 1981.

Marling, Karal Ann. *The Colossus of Roads: Myth and Symbol Along the American Highway.* Minneapolis: University of Minnesota Press, 1984.

Ducks and Decorated Sheds

Andrews, J. J. C. *The Well-Built Elephant and Other Roadside Attractions.* Foreword by David Gebhard. New York: Congdon and Weed, 1984.

Hirshorn, Paul, and Steven Izenour. *White Towers.* Cambridge, Mass.: MIT Press, 1979.

Venturi, Robert, Denise Scott Brown and Steven Izenour. *Learning from Las Vegas: The Forgotten Symbolism of Architectural Form.* 1972. Rev. ed. Cambridge, Mass.: MIT Press, 1977.

Estates

Closs, Christopher W. *Preserving Large Estates.* Information Series, no. 34. National Trust for Historic Preservation. Washington, D.C.: Preservation Press, 1982.

Kaiser, Harvey H. *Great Camps of the Adirondacks.* Boston: David R. Godine, 1982.

Owens, Carole. *The Berkshire Cottages: A Vanishing Era.* Englewood Cliffs, N.J.: Cottage Press, 1984.

Shopsin, William C., and Grania Bolton Marcus. *Saving Large Estates: Conservation, Historic Preservation, Adaptive Reuse.* Setauket, N.Y.: Society for the Preservation of Long Island Antiquities, 1977.

Society for the Preservation of Long Island Antiquities. *Long Island Country Houses and Their Architects, 1860–1940.* New York: W. W. Norton, 1986.

Farms

Hubka, Thomas C. *Big House, Little House, Back House, Barn: The Connected Farm Buildings of New England.* Hanover, N.H.: University Press of New England, 1984.

Stilgoe, John R. *Common Landscape of America, 1580 to 1845.* New Haven, Conn.: Yale University Press, 1982.

Stipe, Robert E., ed. *New Directions in Rural Preservation.* Washington, D.C.: U.S. Department of the Interior, 1980.

Tishler, William H. "The Site Arrangement of Rural Farmsteads." Association for Preservation Technology *Bulletin,* February 1978.

Watson, A. Elizabeth, and Samuel N. Stokes. *Rural Conservation.* Information Series, no. 19. National Trust for Historic Preservation. 1979. Rev. ed. Washington, D.C.: Preservation Press, 1984.

Fences

Hart, John Fraser. *The Look of the Land.* Englewood Cliffs, N.J.: Prentice-Hall, 1975.

Hewes, Leslie, and Christian L. Jung. "Early Fencing on the Middle Western Prairie." Association of American Geographers *Annals,* June 1981.

Mather, Eugene Cotton, and John Fraser Hart. "Fences and Farms." *Geographical Review,* June 1954.

Zelinsky, Wilbur. "Walls and Fences." In *Changing Rural Landscapes.* Edited by Ervin H. Zube and Margaret J. Zube. Amherst: University of Massachusetts Press, 1977.

Firehouses

Walker, Harold S., et al. *Heritage of Flames: The Illustrated History of Early American Firefighting.* New York: Doubleday, 1977.

Zurier, Rebecca. *The American Firehouse: An Architectural and Social History.* Photographs by A. Pierce Bounds. New York: Abbeville Press, 1982.

Forts

Brice, Martin. *Stronghold: A History of Military Architecture.* New York: Schocken, 1984.

Robinson, Willard B. *American Forts: Architectural Form and Function.* Urbana: University of Illinois Press, 1977.

Gas Stations

Vieyra, Daniel I. *"Fill 'Er Up": An Architectural History of America's Gas Stations.* New York: Collier Books, Macmillan, 1979.

Hospitals

Thompson, John D., and Grace Goldin. *The Hospital: A Social and Architectural History.* New Haven, Conn.: Yale University Press, 1975.

Veterans Administration. *The Nation Builds for Those Who Served: An Introduction to the Architectural Heritage of the Veterans Administration.* Washington, D.C.: Veterans Administration and the National Building Museum, 1980.

Houses

Andrews, Wayne. *Architecture, Ambition, and Americans: A Social History of American Architecture.* 1955. Rev. ed. New York: Free Press, Macmillan, 1978.

Foley, Mary Mix. *The American House.* New York: Harper and Row, 1981.

McAlester, Virginia, and Lee McAlester. *A Field Guide to American Houses.* New York: Alfred A. Knopf, 1984.

Moore, Charles W., Donlyn Lyndon and Gerald Allen. *The Place of Houses.* 1974. Rev. ed. New York: Holt, Rinehart and Winston, 1979.

Moore, Charles W., Kathryn Smith and Peter Becker, eds. *Home, Sweet Home: American Domestic Vernacular Architecture.* Craft and Folk Art Museum. New York: Rizzoli, 1983.

Walker, Lester. *American Shelter: An Illustrated Encyclopedia of the American Home.* Preface by Charles Moore. New York: Overlook Press, Viking, 1981.

Indian Settlements

Easton, Bob, and Peter Nabokov. *Native American Architecture.* London and New York: Oxford University Press, 1988.

Reader's Digest Association. *America's Fascinating Indian Heritage.* New York: Random House, 1978.

Sturtevant, William C., ed. *Handbook of North American Indians.* 6 vols. to date. Washington, D.C.: Smithsonian Institution Press, 1978–.

Industrial Structures

Baker, T. Lindsay. *A Field Guide to American Windmills.* Norman: University of Oklahoma Press, 1985.

Fox, William, Bill Brooks and Janice Tyrwhitt. *The Mill.* Boston: New York Graphic Society, 1976.

Hudson, Kenneth. *The Archaeology of Industry.* New York: Scribner's, 1976.

———. *World Industrial Archaeology.* Cambridge: Cambridge University Press, 1979.

Kidney, Walter C. *Working Places: The Adaptive Use of Industrial Buildings.* Society for Industrial Archeology. Pittsburgh: Ober Park Associates, 1976.

Sande, Theodore Anton. *Industrial Archeology: A New Look at the American Heritage.* Brattleboro, Vt.: Stephen Greene Press, 1976.

Starbuck, David R., ed. *An Introductory Bibliography in Industrial Archeology.* Washington, D.C.: Society for Industrial Archeology, 1983.

Weitzman, David. *Traces of the Past: A Field Guide to Industrial Archaeology.* New York: Scribner's, 1980.

Libraries

Bobinski, George S. *Carnegie Libraries: Their History and Impact on American Public Library Development.* Chicago: American Library Association, 1969.

Lushington, Nolan, and Willis N. Mills, Jr. *Libraries Designed for Users.* Hamden, Conn.: Library Professionals Publications, 1980.

Pater, Alan F., and Jason R. Pater, eds. *The Great Libraries of America: A Pictorial History.* Beverly Hills, Calif.: Monitor Book Company, 1981.

Lighthouses

Holland, F. Ross, Jr. *America's Lighthouses: Their Illustrated History Since 1716.* 1972. Rev. ed. Brattleboro, Vt.: Stephen Greene Press, 1981.

Snow, Edward Rowe. *The Lighthouses of New England.* New York: Dodd, Mead, 1984.

Witney, Dudley. *The Lighthouse.* Boston: New York Graphic Society, 1975.

Main Streets

Jackle, John A. *The American Small Town: Twentieth-Century Place Images.* Hamden, Conn.: Archon Books, 1982.

Lingeman, Richard. *Small Town America: A Narrative History 1620–The Present.* New York: G. P. Putnam's Sons, 1980.

Longstreth, Richard. *The Buildings of Main Street.* Washington, D.C.: Preservation Press, 1987.

Reps, John W. *The Making of Urban America: A History of City Planning in the United States.* Princeton, N.J.: Princeton University Press, 1965.

Rifkind, Carole. *Main Street: The Face of Urban America.* New York: Harper and Row, 1977.

Markets

Burke, Padraic. "Reviving the Urban Market: 'Don't Fix It Up Too Much.'" *Nation's Business,* February 1978.

———. "To Market, To Market." *Historic Preservation,* January–March 1977.

Sommer, Robert. *Farmers Markets of America: A Renaissance.* Santa Barbara, Calif.: Capra Press, 1980.

Prisons

Johnston, Norman. *The Human Cage: A Brief History of Prison Architecture.* New York: Walker, 1973.

McKelvey, Blake. *American Prisons: A History of Good Intentions.* 1936. 2nd rev. ed. Montclair, N.J.: Patterson Smith, 1977.

Rothman, David J. *The Discovery of the Asylum: Social Order and Disorder in the New Republic.* Boston: Little Brown, 1971.

U.N. Social Defense Research Institute. *Prison Architecture.* New York: Nichols, 1975.

Railroad Stations

Alexander, Edwin P. *Down at the Depot: American Railroad Stations from 1831 to 1920.* New York: Clarkson Potter, 1970.

Meeks, Carroll L. V. *The Railroad Station: An Architectural History.* New Haven, Conn.: Yale University Press, 1956.

Educational Facilities Laboratories. *Reusing Railroad Stations, Book Two.* New York: EFL, 1975.

Grow, Lawrence. *Waiting for the 5:05: Terminal, Station, and Depot in America.* Main Street Press. New York: Universe Books, 1977.

Ranches

Ferris, Robert G., ed. *Prospector, Cowhand, and Sodbuster: Historic Places Associated with the Mining, Ranching, and Farming Frontiers in the Trans-Mississippi West.* Historic Sites Survey. Washington, D.C.: National Park Service, U.S. Department of the Interior, 1967.

Johnston, Moira, and Dudley Witney. *Ranch: Portrait of a Surviving Dream.* Garden City, N.Y.: Doubleday, 1983.

Robinson, Willard B. "Colonial Ranch Architecture in the Spanish-Mexican Tradition." *Southwestern Historical Quarterly,* October 1979.

Religious Architecture

Albanese, Catherine A. *America, Religions and Religion.* Belmont, Calif.: Wadsworth, 1981.

Armstrong, Richard, Rev., Cheswick Center. *The Preservation of Churches, Synagogues and Other Religious Structures.* Information Series, no. 17. National Trust for Historic Preservation. Washington, D.C.: Preservation Press, 1978.

Belz, Carl I., Bernard Wax, Gerald Bernstein, Gary Tinterow et al. *Two Hundred Years of American Synagogue Architecture.* Waltham, Mass.: American Jewish Historical Society, 1976.

Egbert, Donald Drew. "Religious Expression in American Architecture." In *Religious Perspectives in American Culture.* Vol. 2, *Religion in American Life.* Edited by James Ward Smith and A. Leland Jamison. Princeton, N.J.: Princeton University Press, 1961.

Kennedy, Roger G. *American Churches.* New York: Stewart, Tabori and Chang, 1982.

Stanton, Phoebe. *The Gothic Revival and American Church Architecture: An Episode in Taste, 1840–1856.* Baltimore: Johns Hopkins University Press, 1968.

Resort Hotels

Chambers, Andrea. *Dream Resorts.* New York: Clarkson Potter, 1983.

Gill, Brendan, and Dudley Witney. *Summer Places.* New York: Methuen, 1978.

Lawliss, Chuck. *Great Resorts of America.* New York: Holt, Rinehart and Winston, 1983.

Limerick, Jeffrey W., Nancy Ferguson and Richard Oliver. *America's Grand Resort Hotels.* New York: Pantheon Books, 1979.

Row Houses

Dingemans, Dennis J. "The Urbanization of Suburbia: The Re-

naissance of the Row House."
Landscape, October 1975.

Kitao, T. Kaori. "The Philadelphia Row House: Is It Peculiarly American, or Even Uniquely Philadelphia?" *Swarthmore Alumni Magazine,* April 1977.

Lockwood, Charles. *Bricks and Brownstone: The New York Row House 1783–1929. An Architectural and Social History.* 1972. New York: Abbeville Press, 1983.

Schoolhouses

Eveleth, Samuel F. *Victorian School-House Architecture.* 1870. Reprint. Watkins Glen, N.Y.: American Life Foundation, 1978.

Fiala, Holly H. *Surplus Schools.* Information Series, no. 32. National Trust for Historic Preservation. Washington, D.C.: Preservation Press, 1982.

Gulliford, Andrew. *America's Country Schools.* Washington, D.C.: Preservation Press, 1984.

Schroeder, Fred E. H. "The Little Red Schoolhouse." In *Icons of America.* Edited by Ray B. Browne and Marshall Fishwick. Bowling Green, Ohio: Popular Press, 1978.

Skyscrapers

Goldberger, Paul. *The Skyscraper.* New York: Alfred A. Knopf, 1981.

Huxtable, Ada Louise. *The Tall Building Artistically Reconsidered: The Search for a Skyscraper Style.* New York: Pantheon Books, 1985.

Jencks, Charles. *Skyscrapers-Skycities.* New York: Rizzoli, 1980.

Mujica, Francisco. *History of the Skyscraper.* 1929. Reprint. New York: Da Capo Press, 1977.

Weisman, Winston. "A New View of Skyscraper History." In *The Rise of an American Architecture.* Edited by Edgar Kaufmann, Jr. New York: Praeger, 1970.

Suburbs

Edwards, Arthur M. *The Design of Suburbia: A Critical Study in Environmental History.* Hamden, Conn.: Shoe String Press, 1981.

Jackson, Kenneth T. "The Crab Grass Frontier: 150 Years of Suburban Growth in America." In *The Urban Experience: Themes in American History.* Edited by Raymond A. Mohl and James F. Richardson. Belmont, Calif.: Wadsworth, 1973.

Stern, Robert A. M., ed., with John Montague Massengale. *The Anglo-American Suburb.* Architectural Design Profile. New York: St. Martin's Press, 1981.

Warner, Sam Bass, Jr. *Streetcar Suburbs: The Process of Growth in Boston, 1870–1900.* Cambridge, Mass.: Harvard University Press, 1962.

Wright, Gwendolyn. *Building the Dream: A Social History of Housing in America.* New York: Pantheon Books, 1981.

———. *Moralism and the Model Home: Domestic Architecture and Cultural Conflict in Chicago, 1873–1893.* Chicago: University of Chicago Press, 1980.

Theaters and Movie Houses

Hall, Ben M. *The Best Remaining Seats: The Golden Age of the Movie Palace.* New York: Clarkson Potter, 1961.

Mullin, Donald C. *The Development of the Playhouse: A Survey of Theatre Architecture from the Renaissance to the Present.* Berkeley: University of California Press, 1970.

Naylor, David. *American Picture Palaces: The Architecture of Fantasy.* New York: Van Nostrand Reinhold, 1981.

———. *Great American Movie Theaters.* Washington, D.C.: Preservation Press, 1987.

Stoddard, Richard. *Theatre and Cinema Architecture: A Guide to Information Services.* Detroit: Gale Research Company, 1978.

Stoddard, Robert. *Preservation of Concert Halls, Opera Houses and Movie Palaces.* Information Series, no. 16. National Trust for Historic Preservation. Washington, D.C.: Preservation Press, 1978.

Valerio, Joseph M., and Daniel Friedman. *Movie Palaces: Renaissance and Reuse.* New York: Educational Facilities Laboratories, 1982.

Vernacular Architecture

Glassie, Henry. *Pattern in the Material Folk Culture of the Eastern United States.* Philadelphia: University of Pennsylvania Press, 1969.

Hindle, Brook, ed. *Material Culture of the Wooden Age.* Tarrytown, N.Y.: Sleepy Hollow Press, 1981.

Moholy-Nagy, Sibyl. *Native Genius in Anonymous Architecture in North America.* New York: Schocken Books, 1976.

Noble, Allen G. *Wood, Brick and Stone: The North American Settlement Landscape.* Vol. 1, *Houses.* Amherst: University of Massachusetts Press, 1984.

Rapoport, Amos. *House Form and Culture.* Englewood Cliffs, N.J.: Prentice-Hall, 1969.

Upton, Dell, ed. *America's Architectural Roots: Ethnic Groups That Built America.* Washington, D.C.: Preservation Press, 1987.

Upton, Dell, and John Michael Vlach, eds. *Common Places: Readings in American Vernacular Architecture.* Athens: University of Georgia Press, 1985.

Wells, Camille, ed. *Perspectives in Vernacular Architecture.* Annapolis, Md.: Vernacular Architecture Forum, 1982.

————. *Perspectives in Vernacular Architecture, II.* Columbia, Mo.: University of Missouri Press, 1986.

Zoos

Fisher, James. *Zoos of the World.* Garden City, N.Y.: Natural History Press, Doubleday, 1967.

Hahn, Emily. *Animal Gardens.* Garden City, N.Y.: Doubleday, 1967.

Hancocks, David. *Animals and Architecture: The Story of Buildings for Animals.* New York: Beekman, 1971.

Zuckerman, Lord, ed. *Great Zoos of the World: Their Origin and Significance.* Boulder, Colo.: Westview Press, 1980.

Information Sources

American Association of
Zoological Parks and Aquariums
Oglebay Park
Wheeling, W. Va. 26003

American Aviation
Historical Society
P. O. Box 99
Garden Grove, Calif. 92642

American Farmland Trust
1717 Massachusetts Avenue, N.W.
Washington, D.C. 20036

American Institute of Architects
1735 New York Avenue, N.W.
Washington, D.C. 20006

American Library Association
Architecture for Public Libraries
Committee
50 East Huron Street
Chicago, Ill. 60611

American Society of
Civil Engineers
Committee on History
and Heritage
345 East 47th Street
New York, N.Y. 10017

Association for the Study of
Afro-American Life and History
1407 14th Street, N.W.
Washington, D.C. 20005

Bureau of Prisons
U.S. Department of Justice
Washington, D.C. 20534

Capitol Historical Society of the
United States
200 Maryland Avenue, N.E.
Washington, D.C. 20515

Council on America's
Military Past
P. O. Box 1151
Fort Myer, Va. 22211

Educational Facilities
Laboratories
Academy for Educational
Development
680 Fifth Avenue
New York, N.Y. 10019

Friends of Cast-Iron
Architecture
235 East 87th Street
Suite 6C
New York, N.Y. 10028

Great Lakes Lighthouse Keepers
Association
P.O. Box 2907
Southfield, Mich. 48037

Interfaith Forum on Religion,
Art and Architecture
1777 Church Street, N.W.
Washington, D.C. 20036

League of Historic American
Theatres
1600 H Street, N.W.
Washington, D.C. 20006

Lighthouse Preservation Society
P.O. Box 736
Rockport, Mass. 01966

National Amusement Parks
Historical Association
P.O. Box 83
Mt. Prospect, Ill. 60056

National Carousel Association
P.O. Box 307
Frankfort, Ind. 46041

National Historic Communal
Societies Association and the
Center for Communal Studies
Indiana State University
Evansville, Ind. 47712

National Park Service, U.S.
Department of the Interior:

Historic American
Buildings Survey
Historic American
Engineering Record
P.O. Box 37127
Washington, D.C. 20013-7127

National Register of
Historic Places
P.O. Box 37127
Washington, D.C. 20013-7127

National Society for the
Preservation of Covered Bridges
c/o Mrs. Arnold L. Ellsworth
44 Cleveland Avenue
Worcester, Mass. 01603

National Trust for Historic
Preservation:

National Main Street Center
1785 Massachusetts Avenue, N.W.
Washington, D.C. 20036

Center for Historic Houses
1785 Massachusetts Avenue, N.W.
Washington, D.C. 20036

Regional Offices

Northeast Regional Office
45 School Street
Boston, Mass. 02108

Mid-Atlantic Regional Office
6401 Germantown Avenue
Philadelphia, Pa. 19144

Southern Regional Office
456 King Street
Charleston, S.C. 29403

Midwest Regional Office
54 West Jackson Boulevard
Suite 1135
Chicago, Ill. 60604

Mountains/Plains Regional
Office
511 16th Street
Suite 700
Denver, Colo. 80202

    Texas/New Mexico Field
    Office
    500 Main Street
    Suite 606
    Forth Worth, Tex. 76102

Western Regional Office
One Sutter Street
Suite 707
San Francisco, Calif. 94104

Public Buildings Service
Historic Preservation Officer
U.S. General Services
Administration
Washington, D.C. 20405

Railroad Station Historical
Society
430 Ivy Avenue
Crete, Neb. 68333

Ranching Heritage Center and
Association
Texas Tech University
P.O. Box 4499
Lubbock, Tex. 79409

Society for Commercial
Archeology
Smithsonian Institution
National Museum of
American History
Room 5010
Washington, D.C. 20560

Society of Industrial Archeology
Smithsonian Institution
National Museum of
American History
Room 5020
Washington, D.C. 20560

Society for the Preservation of
Old Mills
P.O. Box 435
Wiscasset, Maine 04578

Society of Architectural
Historians
1232 Pine Street
Philadelphia, Pa. 19107-5944

Theatre Historical Society
P.O. Box 767
San Francisco, Calif. 94101

The United States Lighthouse
Society
130 St. Elmo Way
San Francisco, Calif. 94127

U.S. Army Center of
Military History
Washington, D.C. 20314

U.S. Coast Guard
Public Information Division
Washington, D.C. 20590

Vernacular Architecture Forum
47 Fleet Street
Annapolis, Md. 21401

Other Books from The Preservation Press

Building Watchers Series

WHAT STYLE IS IT? A GUIDE TO AMERICAN ARCHITECTURE. John Poppeliers, S. Allen Chambers, Jr., and Nancy B. Schwartz, Historic American Buildings Survey. One of the most popular, concise books on American architectural styles, this portable guidebook is designed for easy identification of 22 styles of buildings at home or on the road. 112 pp., illus., biblio., gloss. $7.95 pb.

MASTER BUILDERS: A GUIDE TO FAMOUS AMERICAN ARCHITECTS. Introduction by Roger K. Lewis. Forty major architects who have left indelible marks on American architecture—from Bulfinch to Venturi—are profiled in this entertaining introduction. 204 pp., illus., biblio., append., index. $9.95 pb.

AMERICA'S ARCHITECTURAL ROOTS: ETHNIC GROUPS THAT BUILT AMERICA. Dell Upton, Editor. Ethnic groups from Africans to Ukrainians have shaped the way our buildings look. Highlighted here are 22 groups, featured in heavily illustrated chapters that document the rich ethnic diversity of American architecture. 196 pp., illus., biblio., index. $9.95 pb.

THE BUILDINGS OF MAIN STREET: A GUIDE TO AMERICAN COMMERCIAL ARCHITECTURE. Richard Longstreth. A fresh look at architecture found along America's Main Streets. Building types are documented in this unique guide with numerous illustrations from many towns and cities. 156 pp., illus., biblio., index. $8.95 pb.

ALL ABOUT OLD BUILDINGS: THE WHOLE PRESERVATION CATALOG. Diane Maddex, Editor. This fact-filled book offers a lively, readable mixture of illustrations, sources of help, case histories, excerpts and quotations on 15 major subject areas. 436 pp., illus., biblio., index. $39.95 hb, $24.95 pb.

AMERICA'S CITY HALLS. William L. Lebovich, Historic American Buildings Survey. Two centuries of municipal architecture are captured in this book featuring 500 photographs of 114 city halls in 40 states. 224 pp., illus., biblio., append., indexes. $18.95 pb.

AMERICA'S COUNTRY SCHOOLS. Andrew Gulliford. Captures the historical and architectural legacy of country schools from soddies and frame buildings to octagons and provides ideas for preserving them. 296 pp., illus., append., index. $18.95 pb.

AMERICA'S FORGOTTEN ARCHITECTURE. National Trust for Historic Preservation, Tony P. Wrenn and Elizabeth D. Mulloy. A pictorial overview of preservation, the book surveys in 475 photographs what is worth saving and how to do it. 312 pp., illus., biblio., append. Pantheon Books. $14.95 pb.

ARCHABET: AN ARCHITECTURAL ALPHABET. Photographs by Balthazar Korab. Presents a new way of looking at architecture—by searching for an alphabet in, on and around buildings. Juxtaposes dramatic photographs with quotations by architectural observers from Goethe to Wright. 64 pp., illus. $14.95 hb.

ARCHITECTS MAKE ZIG-ZAGS: LOOKING AT ARCHITECTURE FROM A TO Z.
Drawings by Roxie Munro. An architectural ABC whose whimsical illustrations are paired with easy-to-understand definitions for architecture lovers young and old. 64 pp., 48 drawings, biblio. $8.95 pb.

THE BROWN BOOK: A DIRECTORY OF PRESERVATION INFORMATION. Diane Maddex, Editor, with Ellen R. Marsh. The first directory to provide names, addresses and telephone numbers for some 1,000 key preservation organizations and individuals, plus practical preservation tips. 160 pp., illus., biblio., gloss., index. $17.95 spiral bound.

FABRICS FOR HISTORIC BUILDINGS. Jane C. Nylander. 3rd edition. A popular guide that gives practical advice on selecting and using reproductions of historic fabrics. A key feature is an illustrated catalog listing 550 reproduction fabrics. Also included is a list of manufacturers. 160 pp., illus., biblio., gloss. $12.95 pb.

GOODBYE HISTORY, HELLO HAMBURGER: AN ANTHOLOGY OF ARCHITECTURAL DELIGHTS AND DISASTERS. Ada Louise Huxtable. Foreword by John B. Oakes. These 68 pieces, most originally published in the *New York Times*, cover the classic urban confrontations of the 1960s and 1970s, analyzing the failures and successes and urging us to create more livable cities. 208 pp., illus., index. $14.95 pb.

GREAT AMERICAN MOVIE THEATERS. David Naylor. The first guide to 360 of the most dazzling and historic movie theaters still standing throughout the country. Organized by region, state and city, the entries provide colorful architectural and historical descriptions of these magnificent landmarks. An essay details preservation problems—and solutions—while a coda brings back some of the lost great theaters for a final call. Great American Places Series. 276 pp., illus., biblio., index. $16.95 pb.

GREAT AMERICAN BRIDGES AND DAMS. Donald C. Jackson. The first guide to 300 of the most important and best-known bridges and dams in the United States. Organized by region, state and location, the guide includes historical engineering and architectural information on each bridge and dam, provides an overview of the history of these endangered structures and discusses preservation issues involved in saving them. Great American Places Series. 300 pp., illus., biblio., append., index. $16.95 pb.

THE HISTORY OF THE NATIONAL TRUST FOR HISTORIC PRESERVATION, 1963–1973. Elizabeth D. Mulloy. The story of preservation's rise in the 1960s as well as a record of the National Trust's role. 320 pp., color illus., biblio., append., index. $9.95 hb.

HOUSES BY MAIL: A GUIDE TO HOUSES FROM SEARS, ROEBUCK AND COMPANY. Katherine Cole Stevenson and H. Ward Jandl. A unique history and guide to nearly 450 precut house models—from bungalows to colonials—sold by Sears from 1908 to 1940, capturing the pride and memories of Sears house owners. 368 pp., illus., biblio., index. $24.95 pb.

"I FEEL I SHOULD WARN YOU . . ." HISTORIC PRESERVATION CARTOONS. Terry Morton, Editor; essay by Draper Hill. A unique collection of cartoons that have nipped and nudged to keep the wreckers at bay for more than 150 years. 112 pp., illus. $8.95 pb.

INDUSTRIAL EYE. Photographs by Jet Lowe from the Historic American Engineering Record. Introduction by David Weitzman. Some 120 color and duotone photographs are featured in this album of an industrial America that few people have seen—famous landmarks such as the Statue of Liberty as well as less celebrated bridges, power plants, windmills and dams. 128 pp., illus., biblio. $34.95 hb.

THE OBERLIN BOOK OF BANDSTANDS. Celebrates the picturesque and often exotic structures that were magnets for town and city life across America in the 19th century. Included are some 50 different architectural approaches to a bandstand in Oberlin, Ohio, as well as essays on the history of this quintessential community sculpture. 100 pp., illus., biblio., index. $14.95 pb.

OLD AND NEW ARCHITECTURE: DESIGN RELATIONSHIP. National Trust for Historic Preservation. Twenty well-known architects and preservationists tell how old and new buildings can coexist—giving their own solutions, explaining why others fail, suggesting how design review should work and addressing the legal, aesthetic and practical problems of relating old and new. 280 pp., illus., biblio., index. $29.95 hb, $18.95 pb.

PRESENCE OF THE PAST: A HISTORY OF THE PRESERVATION MOVEMENT IN THE U.S. BEFORE WILLIAMSBURG. Charles H. Hosmer, Jr. A thorough and entertaining account of early preservationists and their landmark achievements, this classic recounts famous battles to save such sites as Mount Vernon and Monticello. 386 pp., illus., biblio., index. $14.95 hb.

PRESERVATION COMES OF AGE: FROM WILLIAMSBURG TO THE NATIONAL TRUST, 1926–1949. Charles B. Hosmer, Jr. A monumental study that is the standard reference work on the subject. Should be required reading for preservationists. 1,291 pp., illus., biblio., chron., index. University Press of Virginia. $37.50 hb.

RESPECTFUL REHABILITATION: ANSWERS TO YOUR QUESTIONS ABOUT OLD BUILDINGS. National Park Service. A "Dear Abby" for old buildings, this handy guide (now in an updated edition) answers 150 of the most-asked questions about rehabilitating old houses and other historic buildings. 200 pp., illus., biblio., index. $12.95 pb.

WALLPAPERS FOR HISTORIC BUILDINGS. Richard C. Nylander. This compact handbook shows not only how to select authentic reproductions of historic wallpapers, but also where to buy more than 350 recommended patterns. Arranged according to historical period, this catalog includes a glossary, reading list and manufacturers' addresses. 128 pp., illus., biblio., append. $12.95 pb.

WITH HERITAGE SO RICH. New introduction by Charles B. Hosmer, Jr. A classic that helped spur passage of the 1966 preservation act, this handsome book shows in dramatic photographs and essays why America's architectural heritage should be preserved. Landmark Reprint Series. 232 pp., illus., append. $18.95 pb.

To order Preservation Press books, send the total of the book prices (less 10 percent discount for National Trust members), plus $3 postage and handling, to: Mail Order, National Trust for Historic Preservation, 1600 H Street, N.W., Washington, D.C. 20006. Residents of California, Colorado, Washington, D.C., Illinois, Iowa, Louisiana, Maryland, Massachusetts, New York, Pennsylvania, South Carolina, Texas and Virginia please add applicable sales tax. Make checks payable to the National Trust or provide credit card number, expiration date, signature and telephone number.